A Woman
Seeking
God

DOROTHY KELLEY PATTERSON

A Woman Seeking God

B&H
PUBLISHING GROUP

Nashville, Tennesee

To those who cleared the way for me to seek God:
Our Parents—
>Mom and Dad Kelley
>Honey and Patée Patterson

To those who have walked with me:
Our Siblings—
>Kathy Kelley
>Charlene Kaemmerling Coe
>Rhonda and Chuck Kelley
>Eileen and Steve Turrentine
>David and Rima Amad

To those who walk after me:
Our Nieces and Nephews—
>Beth, Angie, Perry, Kelley, Claire, and Sarah
>Yaser and Nadia

To those whose crowns I am polishing to lay at the feet of the blessed Jesus:
Our Children—
>Armour Paige and Rachel Patterson
>Carmen Leigh and Mark Howell
Our Grandchildren—
>Abigail Leigh and Rebekah Elizabeth Howell

To the one from whom I have learned the most about seeking God:
My husband Paige—mentor, friend, lover . . .

Contents

Part Three: In Her Celebrations

Part Four: In Her Service to God and Country

Preface

For years I have been convinced that more than anything else women need a word from God. God's Word does speak to the women of this generation with the same clarity and authority by which it spoke to the women of the first century and even to the women living in the Old Testament era. Timeless principles have been tested and proven as they have been appropriated by women throughout every generation.

In these brief meditations I have tried to let God's Word speak to the hearts of women in very practical ways—in personal life, in the home, in celebrations, and in service to God and country. Indeed, God's Word is shared and explained, but I have also included my own personal experiences as well as some very practical applications. Whether you use the book in your quiet time for spiritual renewal, in your relaxation hours for inspiration or entertainment, as a special project for suggesting changes or awakening creativity in your own life, or to give as a gift to a family member or special friend or an acquaintance who needs to feel that someone cares about her.

My special thanks go to B&H Publishing Group, and especially editor Jennifer Lyell, whose idea it was to update this volume; to Jo Ellen Burch and Sherry Poe, who helped with the manuscript in its first printing; to Tamra Hernandez, who assisted with preparing the revised and updated draft; to Keith Ninomiya, who has been ever a reservoir of information on sources and a sounding board for ideas; to my children Armour and Carmen, who, at the time of the original preparation of the manuscript, took on mundane tasks to keep me working and who good-naturedly have provided fabulous illustrations and stories within my laboratory of life; and, most of all, to my husband Paige, who makes me believe that I do have something to say that will be worth hearing for someone on this earth!

Dorothy Kelley Patterson
Pecan Manor
Fort Worth, Texas

PART ONE

In Her Personal Life

1

Returning to Bethel: Renew and Refresh

Located about 12 miles north of Jerusalem near the top of a ridge of hills, the ancient village of Bethel is noted for its springs of excellent water. Bethel occupies a strategic point on the east-to-west route from Jordan to the Mediterranean by way of Jericho. One commentator noted that this village is mentioned more in Scripture than any other except Jerusalem.

The name *Bethel* means "house of God." Genesis 28:19 refers to Bethel as a *maqom* (Hebrew), meaning "sanctuary place." When Jacob fled from Esau, he stopped at Bethel. There he set up a stone, poured oil upon it, and called the name of the place the "house of God," or Bethel, because there God had spoken to him in a dream the night before (Gen. 28:1–22). He described that place as "the gate of heaven" (Gen. 28:17). At a later time Jacob revisited Bethel and renewed his covenant with God as he returned from Padan-aram. Again, at Bethel, the Lord reassured Jacob that his descendants would occupy the land (Gen. 35:12).

Bethel had also been a royal city of the Canaanites and thus the site for their pagan sacrifices. During the period of the divided kingdom, Bethel enjoyed an unprecedented period of splendor and significance, and there Jeroboam erected a temple and set up a golden calf, making it the religious center of his kingdom (1 Kings 12:28–30). According to Amos and Hosea, the blatant idolatries of Bethel were accompanied by terrible moral and religious degradation, against which these prophets issued the most scathing denunciations (Amos 3:14; 4:4).

My husband and I have spent many weeks in Israel across the years. We have frequently traversed the land from Dan to Beersheba. However, Jews do not go through Samaria because of the tremendous hostilities existing among the people who live in the land. Although travel along the West Bank is discouraged, we had a deep desire to visit some of the cities that had been so important to our spiritual forefathers. Therefore, from time to time we have hired an Arab driver and set out northward from Jerusalem toward Samaria.

Although much of the country surrounding Bethel is bleak and barren, punctuated by a succession of stony terraces, we have always been touched by the rugged beauty of the land. Immediately I remember the biblical references to Bethel. Foremost among those is the admonition from Yahweh God to Jacob, "Get up! Go to Bethel and settle there. Build an altar there to the God who appeared to you when you fled from your brother Esau" (Gen. 35:1). Surely these words ring often in the ears of Christians who seek to grow spiritually and to renew their commitments. In fact, every believer must make many trips to "Bethel," seeking the will and direction of the Lord and reaching for His strength and sustenance for the trials and difficulties that inevitably arise in the course of life on this earth.

The "Bethel" experience is always appropriate, especially in the fall months as the return to school comes for many children and young people. This season is also the focus for the renewal of labor for many in the work force; it is the point of kicking off the program for the new church year for congregations, and in former years was the time for revivals in churches across the land.

Will you join me in returning to "Bethel"? First, I have determined to "go up" by pursuing with new zeal the setting apart of a time for prayer and reading the Word—a time for communication with the Lord, a period for me to share my burdens and seek His face and a moment for Him to hear my needs and give me guidance and direction. If you have fallen behind in your reading through the Bible, why not begin even now and determine to read through its pages from Genesis to Revelation during a year's time? (See a suggested Bible reading plan at the end of this book.) Are 30 minutes daily too much time for the Lord?

Second, I am looking at the "house of God" that the Lord has provided for me. Our church membership in the last few decades has been in large churches. For example, while my husband was president of the Criswell College, we were members of our sponsoring congregation—the First Baptist Church of Dallas, Texas—large and with varied programs. It would have been easy to concoct an alibi, "They don't need me. There are many others who could do a better job." Yet, the husband and father of our household instructed our family to devote a portion of our energies to building up the local church, which is so precious to the Lord and so pivotal in winning the world to Christ and in edifying believers. Since my husband traveled in ministry, I had the responsibility of seeing that our children put down deep roots in our home church. Now with an empty nest I usually travel with my husband, but still we depend on the prayers of our home church, and we look forward to the fellowship we do enjoy with them when we can be in Fort Worth.

Therefore, you, too, must continually renew your commitment to support the program and outreach of the church in which you hold membership. Gatherings at the "house of God" should be exciting and inspiring to your spiritual life. Attendance in the worship services, visitation in the outreach program, serving in places of responsibility as requested, praying for your pastor and church staff, giving financial resources to undergird the work of the Lord—your commitment to the "house of God" in which the Lord has directed you to serve provides many kingdom opportunities.

Third, I do not want to make my going up to Bethel a whim of the moment, a happenstance, a passing fancy. Rather, I want to live and dwell with the Lord. I want a new and more Christlike lifestyle. I want the Bethel experience to be ongoing, a perpetual sustenance to my life—not a meaningless habit but a meaningful commitment, not a legalistic rule but a heartfelt response, not a man-pleasing exercise but a God-pleasing testimony, not an ordinary observance but an extraordinary experience, not a frequent ritual but an established communion.

Last, I am concerned that my return to Bethel be an altar unto God. The Bethel experience has little validity unless it becomes a testimony to the presence of God in my own life and a witness to the power of God in the lives of others. May God grant to each one of us a "Bethel" experience!

2

Are You Tired or Weary?

²⁸Do you not know?
Have you not heard?
Yahweh is the everlasting God,
the Creator of the whole earth.
He never grows faint or weary;
there is no limit to His understanding.
²⁹He gives strength to the weary
and strengthens the powerless.
³⁰Youths may faint and grow weary,
and young men stumble and fall,
³¹but those who trust in the LORD
will renew their strength;
they will soar on wings like eagles;
they will run and not grow weary;
they will walk and not faint. (Isa. 40:28–31)

A radio interview with Gigi Graham Tchividijian, daughter of Billy and Ruth Graham, sparked my imagination with her perceptive statement: "I have seen my mother bone-tired but not weary." Since my undergraduate studies were in English grammar and literature, I have always had a fascination with etymologies and origins of words. Immediately I began to investigate these words, which I had always used interchangeably. Now I was challenged to look at the concept of "weariness" in Scripture.

According to *Webster's Unabridged Dictionary*, the word *weary* describes one who is worn out in terms of strength, endurance, and vigor—one who has lost freshness or usefulness—one who has exhausted her patience, tolerance, or pleasure. The real shocker in *Webster's* definition of *weariness* came with some finer shades of meaning: namely, a "disillusioned note of futility in life," "exhausted by suffering or sorrow, i.e., mentally or spiritually fatigued." Note especially this last phrase exactly as it came from the dictionary. Consider the number of women of little faith who let circumstances bludgeon them to death (Jer. 20:9).

On the other hand, the word *tired* describes one who has been drained of strength and energy, who is obviously worn by hard use, who is devoid of freshness or originality. These explanations of the term "fatigue" further point to a distinct difference between these two closely related concepts. Fatigue is the exhaustion of strength; it is the "loss of power resulting from continued work, which is removable by rest." An understanding of this concept could revolutionize the lives and attitudes of women all over the world and give them a new source of strength and a more dependable weapon to use against one of their bitterest enemies—weariness!

What Makes Women Weary?

Most women think that question has a thousand answers—babies with the earache; preschoolers with unbounded energy and more destructive creativity than any prison inmate; sons and daughters who would rather fight to hold every boundary than to give an inch for peace; teenagers whose rooms should qualify for federal disaster funds and who revel in challenging every parental decision made; husbands who have just died to all responsibilities at home, except to monitor the football games of the season; employers who think a woman has only one full-time job; schools, churches, and community organizations that are happy to overload their one and only volunteer—ad infinitum.

However, these countless surface pressures point to some underlying enemies that lie in wait to catch their feminine prey. *Weariness can come from confusion*—confusion that issues forth in using your energies wrongfully, confusion in discerning the counsel emanating from many sources, confusion in determining which direction to go. Confusion is best defeated by special care in discernment. The book of Proverbs promises that godly counsel is available (Prov. 15:22), while the book of Isaiah warns about the worldly counsel that hinders your seeking the right help (Isa. 47:12–14). God offers protection in providing a sure means of avoiding this debilitating confusion: "Many plans are in a man's heart, but the LORD's decree will prevail" (Prov. 19:21).

Godly counsel is never self-centered; it is not doing things your own way, according to your own feelings, thoughts, and desires (Isa. 57:10). Rather, godly counsel, of course, is

God-centered; it is doing things God's way regardless of what you think, feel, or want. Only God's Word can provide this spiritual counsel (Ps. 119:9–11, 24).

Weariness is also the result of foolishness (Eccles. 10:15). A fool is often called an "idiot," which is derived from a Greek root meaning more literally "one's own." A fool insists upon having his own way (Prov. 12:15).

Weariness is the result of an attitude of self-pity, resulting from a bitterness of soul (Job 10:1; Pss. 6:6; 69:3). When you take your eyes off the Lord and forget His benefits to you, you are leaving yourself vulnerable to weariness, which begins with a tired body but soon marches deep within to sap the soul and spirit. Now, here is the heart of the matter: Weariness is an attitude toward God. "But Jacob, you have not called on Me, because, Israel, you have become weary of Me" (Isa. 43:22).

What Makes God Weary?

God never "grows weary" in His works and ways (Ps. 6:8; Isa. 40:28–31). He is "wearied" only by the iniquities and sins of His creation (Isa. 1:14; 43:24). However, His weariness is not resignation; rather, He is the One who gives strength from an inexhaustible treasure to any weary soul who comes to Him.

Can God Use Weariness?

Physical fatigue is an expression of soul hunger (Isa. 28:12–13), a time of physical weariness that causes a woman to look toward the Creator God to satisfy her body's hunger and thirst for energy. You cannot multiply by zero and get anything but another zero, but in the spiritual realm God can do this and get everything. Salvation, of course, is ultimate rest. Therefore women are reminded through every physical weariness of the satisfaction that comes in knowing the Lord and trusting Him with their weaknesses. Jesus experienced physical weariness (John 4:6). The Savior began by resting His physical body, but then He turned to the Father God and the Holy Spirit for renewal. In the final analysis, only God can give rest (Deut. 25:18–19), and He will not fail.

Physical weariness can be used as a tool of correction: "Neither be weary of his correction" (Prov. 3:11 KJV). When you are bent on doing things in your own way, sometimes God can get your attention only by pulling back His hand of strength so your body slows down for refueling. How often has this happened in my life when self-sufficiency drove me until my physical strength ran out! Then and only then would I look to the Father for direction and help. The very awareness of weakness is the condition for receiving strength (Matt. 5:6). The earth-laden weak are recipients of the heaven-imported strength. Paul glorified God in his infirmities (2 Cor. 12:9–10).

Physical weariness also prepares women for more significant challenges (Jer. 12:5). God is always looking for a woman's faithfulness in small things before increasing her responsibility for bigger things. Just as an athlete must prepare her body by pushing her to endurance and then gradually adding to the demands upon her skill and strength day by day, even so you must add to your life spiritual nurture, which stretches you to the limits day in and day out. Life will never be free from fatigue, but fatigue can free you from the mundane cares of the world and open your heart and soul to the Lord (Eccles. 12:12).

God's Antitoxin for Weariness

An emphasis on the toil involved in work is found in Scripture. In the garden of Eden, before sin entered the world, God gave the man work to do (Gen. 2:15). In fact, He gave him so much work that he needed a helper, which led to the creation of the woman (Gen. 2:18). In addition, clearly weariness will result from labor. God meant for toil or work to result in the benefit of an end product. When the nation Israel toiled in idolatry and grew weary of God's ways (Jer. 9:5–7), she reaped the product of her labor—God's judgment, which manifested itself in drought, famine, and devastation, prohibiting Israel's harvest of the fruits of the land. When women today toil in their own modern-day idolatries, trying to reject and redo God-given roles and responsibilities for what seems more appealing in the contemporary culture, they are going to experience a drought of genuine happiness, cause a famine for the Word of God, and undergo devastation of their homes and families (Isa. 3:4–5, 12; Ezek. 16:17, 44–45).

God has promised to satiate the weary soul and replenish the sorrowful soul (Jer. 31:25). Nevertheless, He will wait for you to seek Him and find the satisfaction and comfort that only He can give. The farmer does not wait for God to plow and sow his field; but having plowed and sown, he waits for God to bestow the blessing of harvest. Women must not wait for God to keep their homes, to inspire their husbands, to nurture their children, to force open the bud of their creativity. Rather, they must be *home workers*, seeking avenues to enhance the shelter and haven of rest for their own families; they must be lovers of their husbands and lovers of their children, giving themselves unselfishly to meet the needs of their families; they must be willing servants of the Lord, presenting to Him their talents and creativity for ministry in home, church, and community. Then God will open the windows of heaven and pour out blessings on a hospitable home, a devoted husband, loving children, and a meaningful ministry.

You, too, can be "bone-tired" but not weary. You, too, can experience fatigue but not with despair. Your body can be operating on low while your spirit and attitude are high; your physical frailties can cause you to miss some earthly fun and fellowship, but your spiritual resources will enable you to grow better and stronger even from the bed of affliction. Being tired is a human affliction and God's tool for discipline and growth; being weary is an excuse for blaming God for your own sinfulness. God changes physical fatigue to spiritual "fatigues" in leading believers to do battle with the devil. You are never too tired for God to refresh; you are never too old for God to renew.

3

Fatigue—Every Woman's Enemy

He makes me to lie down in green pastures. (Ps. 23:2 NKJV)

Some years ago, my godly husband, in his zeal to give himself to God and ministry, poured out his energies and time beyond all endurance. His tired and broken body simply rebelled. After several weeks of illness at home, he was hospitalized, protesting all the way. A perceptive family member sent a message of concern that read simply, "He maketh me to lie down" (Ps. 23:2 KJV). Truer words were never spoken.

Time and again I have experienced that same frustrating "interference," coming always at the height of my good works and busyness in the kingdom—a time-consuming and seemingly useless interruption in a crowded schedule of caring for my family and ministering for the Lord. Suddenly listless, use-less, and alone, I am led by the Lord to lie down. The Lord's plan for making His children to lie down is designed to edify and restore. What does that plan entail?

Freedom from Fear

For God has not given us a spirit of fearfulness, but one of power, love, and sound judgment. (2 Tim. 1:7)

God alone can remove your fears and anxieties. You can become so busy that you cannot see Him and feel His pres-ence ready to calm your panic over unfortunate happenings and release your terror over the uncertainties of life. You are already off to battle, in the pitiful strength of your own inge-nuity, instead of resting in the Lord and letting Him remove fear, giving the power of strength, the patience of love, and the creativity of a sound mind. When fatigue overcomes, the first step is to release your fears and let God energize and renew you for the task.

Contentment with Circumstances

I have learned to be content in whatever circumstances I am. (Phil. 4:11)

When you are overtaken with exhaustion and fatigue, even a tiny molehill becomes an insurmountable mountain. Every problem is like a balloon. With every breath, the prob-lem becomes larger and you become weaker. Yet God wants to give you contentment with your circumstances, a willing-ness to relax and rest in Him.

Victory over Trials

No temptation has overtaken you except such as is common to man; but God *is* faithful, who will not allow you to be tempted beyond what you are able, but with the temptation will also make the way of escape, that you may be able to bear *it*. (1 Cor. 10:13 NKJV)

The divine Shepherd is constantly watching His sheep. He observes their behavior, and He is aware of their testings. God does not leave His children without the resources to resist and overcome trials and tribulations. He has never promised to take you *out* of the problems, but He has promised to guide you *through* them.

Satisfaction of Needs

"I am the bread of life," Jesus told them. "No one who comes to Me will ever be hungry, and no one who believes in Me will ever be thirsty again." (John 6:35)

When your body has spent its last energy, it searches to satisfy the need for renewal of strength. Then God opens the lush, green pasture of His Word and reveals the knowledge of His will through the Holy Spirit in order to offer perfect satisfaction. How beautiful to know that the most exciting reward you will receive during your lying down is a filling with God's Word.

The Enemy Warns as a Friend

God has redirected the enemy's onslaught so that fatigue is a warning that you need time for the re-creation of energies. Many homes have battery-powered smoke detectors. When the batteries are worn out, the detector begins to beep gently, warning that the system must be rejuvenated. Fatigue is a warning system for the body to renew energies.

In looking at the purpose of God to restore your energies and renew your spiritual sensitivities in order to use you more effectively, you can say "Thank You" when He makes you "lie down," especially because you will always find yourself in His "green pastures," which provide the perfect setting in which to reevaluate your commitment as the Lord rejuvenates your spirit and renews your body.

4

Masks Women Wear

Then the LORD God made the rib He had taken from
the man into a woman and brought her to the man.
(Gen. 2:22)

The woman was God's last creation—the crowning touch,
the completion of a perfect fellowship. The able and venerable
commentator Matthew Henry has written, "If man is the
head, then the woman is the crown." Yet the woman has faced
much upheaval and heartache in finding her God-assigned
place through the centuries.

Today, as never before, the Christian woman has choices
to make—marriage and the home or celibacy and a career.
However, some seem to fall by the wayside, choosing another
alternative, a distortion of God's plan, which should be
labeled not *Miss* or *Mrs.* but *mistake!* This third option is
limited neither to maids nor matrons, but to the woman who

hides behind a mask. She is not authentic in her role, nature, or function.

Generally speaking, I see three popular masks. The first is marked by bitterness and resentment and may be labeled *martyrdom*. Included in this group is the single who fears the draft has bypassed her and thus volunteers to pursue any and every man who looks her way. Bitter with her present state, she feels that marriage is the be-all and the end-all of life. If she cannot be married, she might as well end life! Another woman may reject all moral values and seek pleasures without regard for her own self-worth. A wife may turn inward and center on herself and the problems she faces, the happiness she thinks is missing in the mundane tasks of the household, the absence of attentions from her husband for which her heart longs. All these women are open to the springing up of a "root of bitterness" (Heb. 12:15) and fall easy prey to the martyrdom complex since each one feels that she is "giving up something"—namely, her life and happiness—because of unfortunate circumstances.

Another mistake is the woman obsessed with personal rights and lacking self-control. She hides behind the *Epicurean mask*—preoccupied with satisfying personal desires. Her rights can easily become wrongs! Men and women do not become equal merely by taking off their clothes. An orthopedic surgeon once explained to me that if he were blindfolded and led to the operating table and to a patient whose identity was unknown to him, he could look at the open knee and determine whether his subject was male or female.

This woman wants freedom from marriage and commitment; freedom from babies and responsibility; freedom from stereotyped roles and God-given nature; freedom from legalistic morality, which she might replace with free-wheeling license; freedom from unselfish servitude, which she might trade for self-centered domination. Liberation can be liability. The freedom to swear, smoke, drink, curse, kick, bite, or scratch erases the winsome femininity of God's perfect "building"—a creature of limitless beauty and influence.

The third mask is no less dangerous, though perhaps more subtle. The *mask of hypocrisy* strikes, like the rattlesnake, from close proximity and with deadly venom. This woman appears to have every happiness and success. She may well teach a Sunday school class, serve as president of the missionary organization, chair the hospitality committee, receive the volunteer worker-of-the year award; but she systematically and habitually leaves her family's dinner in the oven and a neighbor to welcome home her schoolchildren. Do "her sons rise up and call her blessed," or is she ever there to hear them? Does "her husband also" praise her (Prov. 31:28), or does he have opportunity to observe or enjoy fruit from her labors? Does she fear the Lord or bow to the demands and expectations of others? Can she work within the framework of divinely assigned responsibility and under the umbrella of God-given authority while governed with Holy Spirit-directed priorities, or must she be "her own person"?

No woman need be a mistake because God has designed each of us to be a unique "living letter known and read of all men." One of the Lord's most invigorating challenges to you comes through the apostle Paul as his own personal testimony, "For I have learned to be content in whatever circumstances I am" (Phil. 4:11), and again, "I am ready for anything through the strength of the one who lives within me" (Phil. 4:13 Phillips).

Never in history has there been a more propitious time for women. They are being equipped; they are being challenged. Look ahead to the future and visualize what God's refinement will do for you; absorb yourself in contentment with a ministry available to you here and now. Whether married or single, each woman can be her own best for Him who died for us all.

5

An Attitude of Gratitude

Praise God for the Thanksgiving season! You cannot escape the unique aspects of this "American" holiday dedicated to thankfulness.

Thanksgiving is a holiday rooted in history. Our forefathers realized that their very existence was the result of divine blessing. The rejection of the land to cultivation, the onslaught of their human opposers, the vengeance of debilitating diseases, and the perils of nature all worked together to discourage, and even eliminate, many of these early settlers.

This holiday is reserved for the family. From its first observance, Thanksgiving has been a time for gathering around the home's table. Whereas Christmas traditionally has been dedicated to the household's children, Thanksgiving is a time for the entire family to join equally in celebration. There is no emphasis on any one generation.

This holiday is devoted to God, transcending the human level not only for the Christian community but also for all who choose to celebrate. The expression of gratitude is to the Creator-Ruler of the universe. Thanksgiving was begun as a national reminder of the blessings of God. Certainly no nation on earth, in any generation, has enjoyed prosperity and blessing equal to or surpassing the United States of America. The spiritual heritage of our God-fearing forefathers has stood the test of time.

What Is Gratitude?

Three essential elements must be present for you to experience gratitude and to express thankfulness. *First, there must be consciousness of the benefit received.* Some years ago I had considerable pain from a ganglion cyst in my right hand. After visits to several doctors and multiple attempts to alleviate the problem, I became convinced that surgery was the only answer. The surgical procedure was minor, or so I thought. However, something went wrong, and for several months after surgery I was in intense pain and virtually lost the use of my right hand. With the help of a patient therapist and the encouragement of a concerned family, I gradually began to regain the use of my hand. Brushing my hair, holding a fork, opening a door—each small task took on new importance; and there was a surging emotion within, an overwhelming sense of gratitude for the smallest task performed with that feeble hand. Never before had I felt genuine gratitude for my hands.

Second, gratitude presupposes contentment, which explains the apostle Paul's admonition (Phil. 4:11). Unless you are pleased with your situation, you will develop bitterness and resentment. A woman of faith who has committed her life to Jesus Christ—the "blessed controller of all things"—may experience loss but not emptiness, disappointment but not despair, adversity but not defeat, because she knows that ultimate victory is coming through Christ (see Rom. 8:28; 1 Cor. 15:57). Three times Paul asked the Lord to remove his "thorn in the flesh," but every time God answered, "My grace is sufficient" (2 Cor. 12:7–9). Believers throughout the world have experienced spiritual growth that ensues only through suffering. Elisabeth Elliot has been twice widowed. She has endured the brutalities of the Ecuadorian jungles; yet she has been a victorious, happy, and grateful woman.

Third, genuine gratitude will find its expression in public acknowledgment or celebration for human kindness and ultimately for divine goodness. There are many expressions of gratitude in Scripture—for food (John 6:11, 23), for wisdom (Dan. 2:23), for personal salvation (2 Cor. 9:15), for a child (Gen. 21:6–7; 1 Sam. 1:27–28), for the privilege of completing a task (Neh. 12:31, 40), for changed lives (1 Thess. 2:13), for God's presence (Ps. 75:1), for the working of God in others (1 Thess. 1:2), for answered prayer (John 11:41), for God's unlimited goodness (Pss. 106:1; 107:1; 136:1–3), for victory (1 Cor. 15:57).

Three decades ago my heart was as full of thanksgiving as it had ever been as I stood on the banks of the Jordan River in Israel. At my side stood our tall eleven-year-old son, who had only a few months before completed his first missionary journey. In the river stood my godly husband leading our young daughter through the waters of baptism. Yes, my gratitude was for answered prayer, for a priceless convert who is now my sister in Christ, as well as my very own daughter;

for a spiritual victory in public testimony of commitment, for a changing life in which Christ is working, for completing the task of bringing our children to faith in Christ. That special time was a public celebration of divine goodness for our family.

What Is an Attitude of Gratitude?

An attitude of gratitude should be part of your lifestyle. It is not dependent upon people or circumstances but rather upon a confident faith in the Lord (Phil. 4:6). The apostle Paul further suggests that this spirit of thanksgiving is to accompany all you do as a testimony for the Lord Jesus to others and as an offering of love to the Father (Col. 3:17). This attitude of gratitude is an essential part of the believer's preparation for coming before the Lord (Pss. 95:2; 100:4), and it is certainly going to be a part of our heavenly abode (Isa. 51:3; Rev. 7:12).

Thanksgiving is not optional, merely chosen as an outfit for the day, but rather it is predetermined as an essential part of the worship of the Lord God (Ps. 50:14). Undoubtedly at times thanksgiving will accompany a sacrifice, even as it did in Old Testament times (Ps. 116:17).

There are times when your thanksgiving must come from a grief-stricken heart, suffering body, or burdened mind, but underlying all human tragedy for the believer is the loving heavenly Father (2 Thess. 2:13). The exhortation of Ephesians 1:6 and 5:20 is for unceasing thanksgiving, especially in your prayers to the heavenly Father.

Biblical Examples of Gratitude

Heading the list of the grateful are the redeemed of the ages (Ps. 107:1–2). You cannot help feeling a thankful spirit when considering the mercy and grace of God and His matchless gift, which provides atonement and payment for your sins. The righteous of every age give thanks to the One who made possible their righteousness and redemption. In the Old Testament is found King David's praise to *Yahweh* God for the opportunity to prepare for the building of His temple (1 Chron. 29:13). In the New Testament, praise flowed from the lips of the prophetess Anna as she beheld the Messiah in human flesh (Luke 2:38). Out of the many who experience healing from Jesus, only a few express gratitude (Luke 17:12–19). There is also the example of Jesus Christ Himself (Matt. 11:25; 26:27; John 11:41) and of the choir of the heavenly host, of which all believers will be a part as they join in the celestial melodies.

The Earthly Challenge

There is no better season of the year to challenge your hearts to godly gratitude than Thanksgiving. You have gone through another year with God's blessings and care surrounding you. Even in the rough times, when you look to Him, you will find the strength and comfort to go on in the race He has set before you. Accept the challenge of the mighty apostle Paul, "Give thanks in everything," for surely this *is* God's will for each one of His children (1 Thess. 5:18).

6

Establishing Priorities: Who's on First?

In 1978, two national football teams were named #1—one sports poll picked the University of Alabama, and another identified the University of Southern California. Fans were frustrated because no group could boast the unequivocal victory; both teams were disappointed because neither team could claim an uncontested title; players had to swallow a bitter pill because the glory sought and earned was stolen; and the world was confused because there was not a *#1!*

Assign God First Place in Your Life

The first step in developing the right priorities is to assign God first place in your life (Matt. 6:33). Manuel Scott suggested that God is often pushed into the background as if He were in the "rumble seat" of a car. Scott exclaimed, "If you don't let God drive, He won't ride."

Jesus set priorities according to His view of the heavenly Father's overall goals. He even said "no" to some of the seemingly good demands placed upon Him if those demands did not fit the Father's overall plan (Luke 4:42–43).

Commune with God Regularly in Your Quiet Time

God's communication with you is dependent upon your giving Him a part of every day. The "quiet time" allows opportunity for God to speak to you through His written Word and permits two-way communication through prayer (Pss. 119:97–104; 55:17). During those quiet moments with the heavenly Father, you can discern among the choices presented and determine the direction to follow.

Note again the example of Jesus in His regular withdrawal from ministry in order to pray (Luke 5:14–16). Jesus always had enough time to do all of God's will for each day (John 17:4). You can find that same victory and satisfaction if you learn to discern the Father's will and determine the tasks to be completed in doing that will.

Evaluate and Improve Yourself

There is an occasion for everything, and a time for every activity under heaven. (Eccles. 3:1)

- *Examine how you spend your time*, which takes concentration and consideration.
- *Plan ahead.* Nothing is so helpful and efficient in budgeting time segments and accounting for time

expenditures as using a planning calendar to apportion the available time according to the demands upon it.

- *Organize your household.* Do away with clutter and assign a place for everything and everything a place.
- *Streamline your work.* Seek shortcuts by studying each procedure with a critical and discerning eye, making an effort for maximum efficiency. Learn to delegate assignments to those who help you.

The Challenge Is *Today*

Above all else, right priorities and good time management demand an awareness that *today* is the only time with which you know you have to work. The past is irretrievably gone, and the future is only a possibility. Do not procrastinate. Begin right now to follow biblical principles in determining how you spend your time. An anonymous philosopher once wrote:

Yesterday is a canceled check.
Tomorrow is a promissory note.
Today is ready cash. Use it.

7

Dealing with Adversity

If you do nothing in a difficult time,
your strength is limited. (Prov. 24:10)

Adversity is defined as "a condition of hardship or affliction, misfortune or calamity." Perhaps a more practical definition would be: Anything too big for us to handle on our own
is adversity. No one is free from adversity—not the rich and
powerful, not the poor and lowly, not the agnostic or atheist,
not the clergyman or saint.

Perhaps the first question in your mind is this: Why does
God allow adversities in the lives of His children? Begin with
the key world *allow*. God's directive will is His determined,
willful action, while His permissive will is that which He
allows with the momentary lifting of His protecting hand.
The picture suggests a parent teaching his young toddler to
walk. If the child is ever to go it alone on his own two feet, he

must be free from parental holding. Yet every parent knows that when he first releases the child to his own power, the child will fall—perhaps repeatedly. That is part of the learning and growing process. So it is in your spiritual life. There will be valleys between the mountains, difficulties en route to victories.

Consider the Believer

God has balanced prosperity with adversity as a reminder to be totally dependent on Him. In your own strength, *You are lacking* (Eccles. 7:13). On the other hand, there is a constant reminder, *You are also worthy*, and thus recipients of mercy and compassion (Heb. 13:3). It is, as you have often heard, "God don't make no junk!" Furthermore, *You are able* (1 Cor. 10:13; Phil. 4:13). God never allows you to enter a valley that is too deep to cross or to enter a night that is too dark to see, nor does He allow you to carry a burden you cannot bear. Most important of all, Jesus, your elder brother, is first and foremost "a brother is born for a difficult time" (Prov. 17:17). Finally, *You are loved* (Rom. 8:37–39). There is no support or strength that is as strong as love, and God's love is perfect, unconditional, and all-consuming.

Remember the Creator

God knows you (Ps. 31:7). After all, He is the Creator and Designer. He is the expert in your nurture and growth. *God cares for you* (Heb. 12:5–6). Chastisement or discipline is an evidence of love because it is essential to growth. *God has confidence in you* (1 Pet. 3:15). Out of the context of suffering often emerge your best opportunities for testimony.

The story of the Englishman John Merrick, known as "The Elephant Man" because of his horrible deformities, was tragic beyond words. His mother was a Baptist; and before her untimely death, she evidently nurtured the faith of her pitiful son. One could not read the book or see the movie without empathetically suffering with this despised man. Yet John Merrick had a most triumphant word when his doctor sorrowfully apologized to him for all that had befallen him. Merrick responded, "Doctor, do not apologize. I am happy every hour of the day."

To me, those words from Merrick's lips seemed impossible. After all, he lived in the most hopeless adversity every minute of the day. Surely God must have had a tremendous confidence in John Merrick, knowing that this young man would have a faith strong enough to sustain him through the deepest tragedies.

God teaches you (Heb. 12:11), and there is no better classroom than adversity. My husband once explained, "Our adversities are God's universities." *God redeems you* (2 Sam. 4:9). Redemption has a past, present, and future tense. You are redeemed from destruction once and for all at conversion; you are redeemed again and again from daily adversities; you will be redeemed at His appearing to spend all eternity with Him.

Are You Willing to Do Your Part?

The first step in overcoming adversity is to *thank God* (Eph. 5:20)—not for the adversity itself, but for the lessons to be learned therefrom and the good that God has promised to bring out of tragedy (Rom. 8:28). Then, you are to *examine yourself* (Ps. 139:23–24).

Are your priorities as they should be? Is your faith anchored in the unchanging God or in the fickle men and women around you? Is your commitment to God *because* of prosperity or *in spite of* adversity?

Finally, you are to *look to God* (Ps. 56:9–11). Although not easy, living by faith is essential. It is the only weapon for adversity that cannot fail (see 2 Cor. 4:8–18) and that is never outdated, never inadequate, never subject to confiscation by the enemy, never without ammunition, never destructive.

8

Testing: The Crucible of Change

No woman escapes the testing of the tempter. Satan appeared first to the woman. The pattern he used to ensnare her, and after her all the generations to follow, is carefully laid out in Scripture. There is no variation in the pattern, but there is tremendous deviation in adapting that pattern to every lifestyle and to any circumstance, and even to every individual's particular weakness.

In Genesis 3:1–6 the deceiver's plan is unveiled. The first step cannot be bypassed. Here every believer has the opportunity to refute the evil one. Satan would be absolutely powerless if you were to refuse your consent; he cannot coerce you into doing wrong. However, neither will God force you into doing right. Everyone has a choice.

Questioning God

Satan's first ploy is to undercut and undermine the Word of God, "Did God really say . . . ?" (Gen. 3:1). The truths of Scripture are your arsenal against the deceiver, who can refute the absolute truth of God as recorded in His Word and as preserved through the generations.

Every temptation begins with questioning the authority of the Bible and casting doubt about the relevance of God's Word. As a woman, I have felt this testing intensively, especially during recent decades in which there has been an attempt to erase the divinely given role assignments within the home. Did God really say that I am to be submissive to my husband even when he is wrong? What if my husband does not handle money responsibly? What if he is not attentive to the children? What if he is not a good leader?

Whether by distortion, doubt, or outright denial, Satan entices you to ignore the clear teaching of Scripture. I am committed to the absolute authority of every word of Scripture as inerrant (without error and infallible) if for no other reason than because of the collapse of homes that are self-destructing around you. Such could not have happened even if only those in the Christian community were so committed to biblical authority that they maintained divinely assigned roles within the family.

Contradicting God

"No! You will not die" (Gen. 3:4). The inevitable result of your questioning God's Word is the ultimate contradiction of

His Word. Some will second-guess God with rationalizations like these:

- "God did not say that I have to live with a man whom I no longer love or respect."
- "God did not say that I have to move with my husband away from my family and friends."
- "God wants me to be happy the way I think I will be happy."
- "God really would not say something illogical and outdated, or if He had, the changes in time and culture would have negated it, and the lack of scientific confirmation would have proven it invalid."

The worst flaw in this reasoning is that a mere human being is sitting in judgment upon the Lord of the universe. The creature wants to appear more enlightened than the Creator. Civilization and education, according to this humanistic rationalization, are more enriching than the truths of God.

Surpassing God

Satan's next step is to suggest some imaginary good above and beyond what God has offered in His Word: "You will be like God" (Gen. 3:5). In other words, Satan appears more beneficent than God. The immediate, pleasurable effect of the forbidden hides the inevitable, deadly result of ignoring God's Word.

How tragic to view God's children caught in this vicious trap, eagerly seeking something "better than God's best." Adam and Eve were living in paradise—no difficulties, no

trials, no sorrows. They had perfect fellowship, perfect intimacy, perfect harmony; yet Satan convinced them that he
could offer something better. That something better turned
out to be adding toil to work, attaching pain to childbirth,
introducing murder to the family circle. Likewise, every sin is
a senseless and superstitious belief in the supposedly beneficial effects of sin.

9

Prayer Power: Court of Complaint or Pipe for Power

[1]God, listen to my prayer
and do not ignore my plea for help.
[2]Pay attention to me and answer me.
I am restless and in turmoil with my complaint,
[3]because of the enemy's voice,
because of the pressure of the wicked.
For they bring down disaster on me
and harass me in anger.

[4]My heart shudders within me;
terrors of death sweep over me.
[5]Fear and trembling grip me;
horror has overwhelmed me.

[6]I said, "If only I had wings like a dove!
I would fly away and find rest.
[7]How far away I would flee;
I would stay in the wilderness.

Selah

[8]I would hurry to my shelter
from the raging wind and the storm."

[9]Lord, confuse and confound their speech,
for I see violence and strife in the city;
[10]day and night they make the rounds on its walls.
Crime and trouble are within it;
[11]destruction is inside it;
oppression and deceit never leave its marketplace.

[12]Now it is not an enemy who insults me—
otherwise I could bear it;
it is not a foe who rises up against me—
otherwise I could hide from him.
[13]But it is you, a man who is my peer,
my companion and good friend!
[14]We used to have close fellowship;
we walked with the crowd into the house of God.

[15]Let death take them by surprise;
let them go down to Sheol alive,
because evil is in their homes and within them.
[16]But I call to God,
and the LORD will save me.
[17]I complain and groan morning, noon, and night,
and He hears my voice.
[18]Though many are against me,
He will redeem me from my battle unharmed.

¹⁹God, the One enthroned from long ago,
will hear and will humiliate them   *Selah*
because they do not change
and do not fear God.

²⁰My friend acts violently
against those at peace with him;
he violates his covenant.
²¹His buttery words are smooth,
but war is in his heart.
His words are softer than oil,
but they are drawn swords.

²²Cast your burden on the LORD,
and He will sustain you;
He will never allow the righteous to be shaken.

²³God, You will bring them down
to the Pit of destruction;
men of bloodshed and treachery
will not live out half their days.
But I will trust in You. (Ps. 55:1–23)

This psalm of lament is a prayer in the midst of a wicked conspiracy involving a formerly trusted friend. The first section of the psalm (55:1–8) pours forth in anguish the complaint about the author's enemies. The second section (55:9–11) calls for judgment upon the evildoers. The third section (55:12–15) focuses on the false friend who has found a place in the company of the enemy. A person with whom the psalmist had sweet counsel and who joined him in worship of God now was seeking to destroy him.

Your minds immediately turn to Judas, one of the inti-mate band of disciples, one who was close to the Savior, one who sat under His teaching and observed His miracles, one who felt His heartbeat, and yet one who turned on Him and turned over the blessed Savior to the enemies who sought His life. This psalm surely was relived in vivid detail in the life of the Lord Himself.

In the fourth section, verses 16–23 express confidence in the Lord's help. Herein you find life as a challenge for continual exercise of prayer (55:16–17), as an opportunity for repeated delivery from dangers (55:18), and as the confident assurance of future protection and guidance (55:22–23).

The Beginning of the Day

The Hebrew day began in the evening. In the creation account you will find the expression, "Evening came and then morning" (Gen. 1). The custom of prayer for the devout Hebrew involved prayer three times—once at each time of change. Evening, morning, and noon presented the day in its whole cycle.

Daniel's conduct was indicative of devout commitment. Israelites who habitually offered prayer three times a day (Dan. 6:10). This practice began with the prayers associated with the morning and evening sacrifices (Exod. 29:38–42) and later included the midday. There is also an exciting expression of incessancy in the determination to lay matters before God, not only unceasingly in the solemn quiet of your own spirit but also in utterances at specific times throughout the day.

For every Christian there is also a unique meaning in the evening, morning, and noon cycle. The Lord Jesus died on the cross in the dark of the evening. He arose from the grave, conquering death, in the glorious morning glow; and at the midday He is standing before the Father in intercession for His redeemed.

The Assurance of a Deliverer

The crisis or turning point (55:16) came when the psalmist recognized that, though he could not flee from his enemy with promise of escape, he could seek refuge in God with the assurance of deliverance. In the midst of an unjust and cruel world, there is still the eternal righteousness, infinite love, and divine faithfulness of the heavenly Father. Here the psalmist called upon God as *Elohim*—the One who is exalted above the world, the Creator, the Almighty Ruler of the universe; but note the change in the use of names when the psalmist identifies the one from whom the answer came as *Yahweh* (the personal name of God, which the devout Hebrew will not utter even today)—the One who mercifully interposes in the history of the world, the Deliverer, the Covenant God, the self-existent One in whom Israel trusted.

The psalmist, though still grieved by his unfaithful friend, has turned altogether to God. He addresses *Yahweh* and expresses the confidence that God will continue to answer his prayers by coming to his aid, delivering his soul, and visiting his enemies with affliction and destruction.

10

Prayer: The Classroom for Faith

I complain and groan morning, noon, and night,
and He hears my voice. (Ps. 55:17)

Practically speaking, there are several exciting lessons to learn in the prayer pattern expressed in Psalm 55:17.

Personal Petition

Prayers must be personal, expressing individual need and heart's desire. The most personal prayers in Scripture present an outpouring through direct petition to God. Note Hannah who prayed and wept before the Lord, pleading for a child. She expressed her heart's desire clearly and earnestly.

Confident Expectation

Prayer ought to be offered in faithful confidence. "But I call to God, and the LORD will save me" (Ps. 55:16). Mary, chosen to be the mother of the Lord Jesus, prayed in quiet confidence: "May it be done to me according to your word" (Luke 1:38). Despite the difficult days ahead, Mary then praised the Lord and waited for Him to meet her needs. You must trust the providence of God to fulfill even our most mundane necessities.

Grateful Testimony

Not only in this psalm, but in others as well, there is the encouragement to cry aloud unto the Lord. Anna's prayer of thanksgiving in the temple as she saw Messiah was voiced aloud so that all of those around her could hear her joyous testimony to the Lord.

Appointed Time

Prayer is offered throughout the day. Definite quiet times for communion with God the Father are set aside. Perhaps the evening prayer is a period for meditation and refreshment; the morning prayer, a time for strength and creativity in the new opportunities; and the noontime, a pause for dealing with that day's particular problems.

Daily Challenge

Prayer is also offered seasonally. For example, the fall has traditionally been a time of renewal and revival in churches across the land. The returning of children to school, the resuming of disciplined schedules after family vacations and leisure, the changing of the season—all these factors affect life and family. What an appropriate time to examine your relationship to the heavenly Father, to recommit yourself to the spiritual nurture of a daily devotional time, and to set the example for doing so before your children.

Women, you will find your responsibilities more rewarding, your burdens lighter, your satisfactions more fulfilling, your lives more enriched and meaningful when you pray evening, morning, and at noon. You then keep the Lord close as you walk through your day, enjoying His presence continually and having His guidance consistently.

11

Learning: A Journey through the Seasons of Life

In Ecclesiastes wise Solomon tells the truth about life lived apart from God: It is the pits! Such a life is marked by emptiness (1:2, 9, 14), by distortion of the good (wisdom becoming grief, and knowledge ebbing into pain, 1:18), by preoccupation with pleasure-seeking (a futile and profitless venture, 2:1–2), and by oppressive labor (grievous, wearisome, pointless toil, 2:11).

Everything Is Timely

Believers desire to see the kingdom of God established, but they must wait for that timing as it has been set in the councils of God. The efforts of the Pharisees to seize Jesus were fruitless until His hour arrived (see John 7:30). Blind fate is no match for the purposeful planning of the compassionate, gracious, long-suffering Father whose vast love and faithfulness overwhelm judgment with mercy.

God is the ultimate Controller of time (see Eccles. 3:11; 8:5–7). When my children began their participation in athletics during junior high and high school years, I felt in my heart that the Lord was redirecting me. Canceling my speaking engagements and giving up ministries in the churches with my husband, I focused my energies and creativity in a new way upon my teenagers. Making such radical changes was not easy, but God has reconfirmed again and again that this decision was His best for me during that season of my life. Some warned that I would not have future opportunities to speak if I rejected invitations for five years, and the invitations did quickly all but cease. However, almost to the day my daughter graduated from high school they began to come again. The Lord opened more doors than ever before; another season had begun.

Every woman is a steward of the time God gives (see Eph. 5:15–16). The allotting of time, that measurable period during which events occur, involves process and change. Time cannot be recaptured or relived, which makes it imperative that you use it wisely and according to divine plan.

Everything Has Purpose

In Ecclesiastes 3:2–8, God expresses His purposes via a series of contrasts. Multiples of seven indicate completeness, and these verses contain 14 pairs of opposites. This interesting literary device, called "merism," is one in which polar opposites are used so that each cancels out the other to suggest totality. Life and death present the whole view since death is a passage to life (see Ps. 78:3–4). Planting and harvest are both necessary to cultivate growth.

Killing and healing are but confirmations that life is a mixture of battlefields and first-aid stations. God's corrective measures may be so rigorous that they are designated as slayings. Again and again in my own life I have been reminded of the words of the psalmist, "He makes me to lie down" (Ps. 23:2 NKJV), when in exhaustion or sickness I have been forced to bed, giving both body and spirit a time to refuel. Breaking down and building up suggest that God pulls down and destroys as a means of building just as the demolition crews must destroy the old edifice before constructing the new. Well do I remember the day for implosion of the old hotel adjoining our church. We hated to see the landmark go, but the parking garage that supplanted it had opened the door for growth and expansion.

Both weeping and laughter can be used by God to get your attention, but few would dispute that suffering is His most effective tool. C. S. Lewis once remarked, "God whispers to us in our pleasures, speaks in our conscience, but shouts in our pains; it is his megaphone to rouse a deaf world."

Mourning and dancing, casting away and gathering, embracing and standing apart are all descriptions of the reactions of the human family. There are times to affirm others and thank them for their encouragement, and there are times when caring confrontation and constructive criticism are needed. At a low point in my own life I was confined to bed in a darkened room unable to function effectively in any area of life. My husband made arrangements for me to fly from New Orleans to Dallas to see a specialist in allergies and asthma.

Although I expected this Christian doctor's sympathy and some kind of super medication to reactivate my worn-out frame, the doctor instead chose caring confrontation, informing me that my body was allergic to my mind and that I could expect to spend the rest of my life as an invalid because of my refusal to accept the physical limitations imposed by my allergies and respiratory complications. At the time I was furious with him for his lack of sensitivity; but, on more mature reflection, I have become grateful to God for the doctor's courage in telling me the truth and challenging me to make necessary changes in my lifestyle.

Gaining and losing suggest that you may have to deprive yourself of some things in order to secure more important goals. Keeping and throwing away refer to the necessity of identifying what is of value to keep while being willing to cast out things no longer useful. Beleaguered sailors were willing to throw away supplies and equipment in order to save their sailing vessels (see Jon. 1:5; Acts 27:18–19, 38).

Rending and sewing suggest the need for mending after garments have been torn as a sign of mourning (see Gen. 37:34). Repentance requires tearing away in order to build anew.

Being silent is contrasted with speaking. Speech is tempered because of the conviction that a time to speak will come (see Job 2:11–13). On the one hand there are times when it is wise, considerate, and loving to be quiet; on the other hand, there is a day for declaring one's convictions boldly whatever the cost (see Prov. 15:23).

Loving and hating form a couplet difficult to understand. The Lord may choose to cause the world to love His people, but He may also lift His protective hand and give them over to the world's hatred. In response to every season of correction comes a time for refreshing, namely, those "showers of blessings."

Peace and war also challenge the Christian. When tyranny threatens just as in the case of Esther and her people, whose destruction was sought by the wicked Haman, war may be a necessary self-defense (Esther 9:1–2). However, when differences can be resolved and rights restored, peace should be sought to avert war, though God never did intend for us to seek peace at any price.

The Purposes of God Differ from Mine

You dare not pass beyond or limit divine providence. Prayer is the believer's tool for altering the times. Repentance with God is not the changing of His will, as with mankind, but rather the willing of a change. Difficulties often provide the setting for wholesome discipline, which constrains you to humble yourself and feel your own insufficiencies. In my life these difficulties found expression in physical maladies that plagued me all through the preparation years my husband and I spent in college and seminary.

God was working in my life within the framework of His master plan (see Eccles. 9:1). Only from His divine perspective could the real meaning and worth of my life be understood. My first season of anguish came after I married a preacher. Debilitating and chronic illness, financial pressures, and the loss of my first baby became God's university for me in the life of faith. At the time, I could only see and react to the tragedy of the moment. My struggle and toil began when my faith and prayer ceased, but the Lord did not give up on me. He led me "*through* the waters . . . *through* the rivers . . . *through* the fire" (Isa. 43:2). Out of my deepest struggles and most oppressive toil arose my strongest faith and most diligent prayer.

Every Work Should Be Profitable

Work is a gift of God. The perfect garden of Eden had work to be done, and heaven will have work. Rather than laboring and scheming, you must learn to enjoy the present toil. The beautiful relationship of God to the world is one of dependence, variety, order. My relationship to the world is different indeed and involves fatigue (no permanent relief from difficulties), ignorance (no perfect knowledge), submission (acceptance of my limitations), and fear (respect for God's creative handiwork). You must transcend the human to see the divine; you must look beyond the sun to view heaven. The ability to enjoy divine blessings is in itself a gift of God (see Eccles. 2:24–26). As a "workaholic," I actively have had to pursue learning simple pleasures (going for a walk, visiting a museum, engaging in conversation, visiting a shopping mall merely to check out the windows and watch the people). You must search for God, not in your own way, but in His way (see Heb. 11:6).

Comforting indeed is the fact that no one can frustrate God's plan without His consent. God's work is perfect and unalterable (see Isa. 46:10); His work is eternal (Ps. 33:11); and He works with purpose (57:2). In the midst of the jarring and fluctuating circumstances of men, God holds all the threads to each life's tapestry. When you examine your life *with* God, the focus changes. Hope, encouragement, and deliverance come to the forefront to move you forward.

> All the world's a stage,
> And all the men and women are merely players:
> They have their exits and their entrances;
> And one man in his time plays many parts,
> His acts being seven ages.
> (Shakespeare, *As You Like It,* Act 2, Scene 7)

A Wise Conclusion in Ecclesiastes

Surrender, submit, and serenely wait on God. Let God exalt *in His season,* whether through prosperity or misfortune. Live for the present moment; cheerfully enjoy its pleasures (3:11); do good (v. 12). Be aware that only God gives deliverance from care (v. 13). Grief and pain in themselves do not alter the eternal counsels of God (v. 14). Everything comes as God foreordained and in His own good time (v. 15).

You can cherish the hope of God's judgment on wickedness (vv. 16–17). The delay of divine intervention allows for your own purifying and humbling, even in the most helpless condition (vv. 18–21). Seeing the uncertainty of the future, you should not trouble yourself about it but relax and prepare to enjoy the future (v. 22), which comes not as the result of blind fate but rather is ordered by the compassionate, gracious, long-suffering, and faithful *Yahweh* God.

> When you are hit with the pits,
> Use more than your wits!
> Go with confidence to the Bible;

God's Word will be found reliable.
His promises are surely there;
The Lord does indeed care.
Upon Him your burdens should fall;
For His help you must call.
He will be faithful to the end—
Your every need He will attend.

Dorothy Kelley Patterson

PART TWO

In Her Home

12

Homemaking as a Chosen Career

Many women today have built their identity upon ambitious busyness in the vocational world, public achievement in the community, and a personal paycheck for investments and financial pursuits. Choices for women have been narrowed to career options outside the home. Cutting the apron strings, women have freed themselves from the mundane responsibilities of rearing children and keeping a home only to be enslaved by computer keyboards and electronic gadgetry; they have been freed from preparing gourmet dinners to defrosting their bland, commercially prepared and chemically preserved menus; and they have been enslaved by the necessity of fighting the traffic to and from home as they embrace new arenas of productivity. Mom and hot apple pie have been replaced by the day-care center and a fast-food apple turnover.

Somewhere along the way in expressing themselves and bettering their lifestyles, women have lost one very satisfying option: to "work" as a homemaker, neither being employed nor wanting to be employed outside the home. In short, many women have come to believe that a woman who devotes her primary energies to the care of home and family is enslaved to failure and boredom in an occupation perceived as unworthy of time and effort and without the support of titled position and monetary compensation.

From Whence Came the Salaried Wife?

In the garden of Eden the tempter began his encounter with the woman by questioning the Word of God, "Did God really say, 'You can't eat from any tree in the garden'?" (Gen. 3:1).

Accordingly, throughout the generations women have faced the tempter at this very point: Does God speak to women concerning their roles and responsibilities? If so, does He mean what He says? I believe the answer is *yes* to both questions. Satan has never ceased to attack believing women at the most vulnerable point. Every woman, as Eve, desires the best for her family *and* for herself. Women want to achieve, and perhaps the most difficult question lies in defining achievement: What criteria are necessary for success? Is being someone's wife and another's mother really worth the investment of a life? Does it take preparation and a skill set, as well as concentration of energy and even creativity, to maintain a home?

Adlai Stevenson once challenged the graduating women of Smith College to "influence us, man and boy," to "restore valid, meaningful purpose to life in your home," and to keep their husbands "truly purposeful." What a different scene today! The emergence of inexpensive, effective birth control measures has cut the size of average families from four children in 1957 to fewer than two since 1991. Women are giving less and less of their time to bearing and rearing children; marriage is being delayed to allow career preparation and pursuit. For too many women, motherhood has become as mechanical and insignificant as the tasks that are performed in a household. Marriage has become a partnership in which household tasks are carefully divided and assigned. Both husband and wife feel compelled to choose careers with the same earning power and opportunity for advancement. Then the mundane household tasks are divvied up. However, as someone quipped, "Everybody is in favor of equal pay, but nobody is in favor of doing the dishes."

What Is a Career?

A career is a profession for which one trains with the purpose of undertaking the venture as a permanent calling. It demands full speed or intense exercise of activity and the pursuit of consecutive, progressive achievement. A career requires training and preparation, commitment and loyalty, energy and time, excellence and achievement. Can you find an efficient, capable person who is professionally adequate in many and varied careers simultaneously? For example, would you want your family doctor to be your postman and policeman as well? No! Why? Because you want your doctor to specialize and sharpen his expertise in the field of medicine! Yet, what doctor has not dictated letters and reports to be mailed to his colleagues? What physician has not sat down with some troubled patient as counselor-adviser? In other words, within most careers a diversity of opportunity is governed by a priority of responsibility. If a doctor makes records, reports, or counseling sessions more important than updating and maintaining his professional skills and if he haphazardly performs his services of evaluating and treating his patients, he will soon have no need to make reports or do counseling—because his patient load will dwindle. In other words, within every career there is specialization in purpose and preparation but generalization in service and opportunity.

The next question is this: Is *homemaking* a career? The dictionary defines the homemaker as "one who manages a household, especially a wife and mother." Why is the homemaking career important enough to demand a woman's foremost commitment, full energies, and greatest creativity?

Keeping the home is an assignment to the wife from God Himself. In Titus 2:3–5, Paul admonished the "older [i.e., spiritually mature] women" to teach the younger (i.e., "new" and "fresh") women to be *lovers of their husbands* (Greek, *philandrous*), *lovers of their children* (Greek, *philoteknous*), and *home-workers* (Greek, *oikourous*). In Proverbs 31, not only is there emphasis upon the woman's responsibility in caring for her household but also upon the scope and magnitude of the homemaker's task. This amazing "woman of strength" (Prov. 31:10–11) was trustworthy, loving, organized, and quite productive while reaching out to her neighborhood and helping the poor (Prov. 31:20) and thereby proving herself worthy of commendation (Prov. 31:31). She used her energies and creativity to administer her household efficiently (Prov. 31:13–16, 18–19, 21, 24, 27). The woman described in this passage may well be the forerunner of the bionic woman!

Many people are surprised to discover how much time is actually required to run a house and care for a family. Some experts have suggested that although our automatic, labor-saving appliances are less demanding on the worker's physical energies, the overall time demands are no less than they were fifty years ago. While an hour may be saved in food preparation and cleanup, an hour is added in marketing, management, errands, and extra-home activities. One must remember that the preparation and care of the shelter for the family is important enough for God Himself to assign that responsibility.

Rearing the next generation is an awesome task. Some women seem to limit parenthood to the labor room, seeking a "maternity sabbatical" in which a few weeks' leave is taken to deliver a baby before rushing back to a career's lofty pursuits. The prophet Ezekiel issued words of warning:

> Moreover you took your sons and your daughters, whom you bore to Me, and these you sacrificed to them to be devoured. . . . Indeed everyone who quotes proverbs will use *this* proverb against you: "Like mother, like daughter!" You *are* your mother's daughter, loathing husband and children; and you *are* the sister of your sisters, who loathed their husbands and children. . . . (Ezek. 16:20, 44–45 NKJV)

A young woman wrote to the "Dear Abby" column, describing her mother as "a professional woman who collected a husband, a daughter, and a dog to *enrich* her life." According to the daughter, the only one not damaged by this *enrichment* was the dog! Using other human beings to fulfill yourself is only worthwhile if you can give as well as take. After all, children are not machines! In an interview, actress Katharine Hepburn said,

> I'm not sure any woman can successfully pursue a career and be a mother at the same time. The trouble with women today is that they want everything. But no one can have it all. I haven't been handicapped by children. Nor have I handicapped children by bringing them into the world and going ahead with my career.[1]

Women need to be educated in the responsibilities of parenthood. To give the task of producing the next generation, the most strategic and demanding assignment in the world, to people without any qualifications whatsoever, and often to those without any motivation for acquiring qualifications and preparation is absurd. "My career has suffered because of the children, and my children have suffered because of my career. I've been torn and haven't been able to function fully in either arena. I don't know one person who does both successfully, and I know a lot of working mothers," said actress Joanne Woodward.[2] Golda Meir, former prime minister of Israel, confessed in her later years that she still suffered nagging doubts about the price her two children paid for her career, adding, "You can get used to anything if you have to, even feeling perpetually guilty."[3] Motherhood, encompassing a lifetime and beyond, is more time-consuming than any full-time job in the world's marketplace. A child needs his mother to be *all* there, to be focused upon him, to recognize his problems and needs; to support, guide, see, listen to him, to love and want him.

The wife was created by God to be a "helper" for her husband. When a wife seeks employment outside the home, her life and the lives of her husband and children are impacted. Suddenly she has added to the task of household management the burden of professional career responsibilities. Her husband may be frustrated because of his wife's fatigue and even the absence of her fellowship since she may often seem to work around the clock over the weekend to catch up at home. Sometimes a man's God-given ego (that innermost drive to provide for the needs and desires of his family) suffers a blow as he experiences the frustration of feeling that he is not providing for his family. A woman's career can easily serve as a *surrogate husband* because her responsibilities during employment hours are dictated by her employer's preference as she works to complete with excellence the tasks assigned to her. A husband often must bend and adapt his schedule for emergencies with the children, visits of repairmen to the home, and so forth, because the addition of responsibilities outside the home causes a wife and mother to lose much of her flexibility for overseeing the household and children.

> Youths oppress My people,
> and women rule over them.
> My people, your leaders mislead you;
> they confuse the direction of your paths. (Isa. 3:12)

One author describes certain professional careers, such as ministers, politicians, administrators, and businessmen, as demanding helpmates for success. These wives must not only maintain an orderly house, keep themselves attractive, become involved in volunteer activities that will benefit their husbands, but also entertain frequently. This description would probably apply to the responsibility and opportunity of every wife. I have often thought that if anyone ever had a reason for bigamy, it would be Paige Patterson! Even a harem could not accomplish all the work he needs to have done!

Too many women rush headlong into a career, determined to waste no time or effort on *housework* or *babysitting* but rather seek to achieve position and monetary compensation by directing all talents and energies toward professional achievement. Golda Meir, by her own testimony, devoted her adult life to the birth and rearing of Israel at the cost of her marriage. She separated from her reticent husband to pursue her public life. To quote Mrs. Meir,

> What I was made it impossible for him [her husband] to have the sort of wife he wanted and needed . . . I had to decide which came first: my duty to my husband, my home, and my child or the kind of life I myself really wanted. Not for the first time—and certainly not for the last—I realized that in a conflict between my duty and my innermost desires, it was my duty that had the prior claim.[4]

Though the *duty* of wifehood and motherhood had claim, the desires of personal ambition and success laid hold, about which the Lord warned:

> But each person is tempted when he is drawn away and enticed by his own evil desires [Greek, *epithumia*, literally "hot after" or "lust"]. Then after desire has

conceived, it gives birth to sin [Greek, *harmartia*, literally "missing the mark"], and when sin is fully grown, it
gives birth to death. (James 1:14–15)

Then the woman saw that the tree was good for food
[appetite] and delightful to look at [beauty], and that it
was desirable for obtaining wisdom [ambition]. So she
took some of its fruit and ate it; she also gave some to
her husband, who was with her, and he ate it. (Gen. 3:6)

Wives and mothers are needed for standing in the gap in fam-
ily emergencies, for volunteers in church and community, and so
forth. What would happen if women returned to the home?
First, most men could find employment, although they might
have to work harder and longer. What would happen if wives
and mothers became excited and enthusiastic about being
homemakers and devoted all their energies and creativity to
assisting their husbands, nurturing their children, making a
success of their marriages and family life? Certainly children
and husbands would enjoy the blessing of this added attention; assuredly the home would come again to the forefront
of society as the "rock from which you are hewn" (Isa. 51:1);
surely divorce, delinquency, and family turmoil would begin
to wane and fade. They would also add a dedicated and talented force of volunteers to support community and church.

Where Do We Go from Here?

These ideas, based on my understanding of the principles
found in God's Word, go against culture and are counter to
the practices of this generation. Yet many families struggle
with too much focus away from home and family. God is

calling the women of this generation to a revival of their commitment of hearts and lives to His creative purposes. If you choose to make this journey, here is a creative prescription to be considered by wives and mothers who have chosen employment outside the home:

1. Renew before God your priority commitment to husband, children, and home.

2. Seek your husband's counsel in the matter. "Dear husband and leader, is my employment outside the home the very best help I can be to you, the children, and our home?"

3. If you receive an overwhelming affirmation that your husband wants you to continue employment for the sake of the family—*not* primarily for your happiness (If you cannot be happy and fulfilled in home ministry, you need to seek the Lord's help through prayer and study of the Word in straightening out your own heart)—then continue, being careful to make every effort to keep your priorities in line.

4. If you husband asks you to retire from employment, then do so sweetly and quickly. Extend your energies and creativities from the home base, beginning with your family circle and extending throughout the community and around the world.

Notes

1. "An Interview with Kate Hepburn," *The Ladies Home Journal,* March 1977, 54.

2. "Joanne and Paul," *The Ladies Home Journal,* July 1975, 62.

3. Books section, *Newsweek,* November 3, 1975, 88.

4. Ibid.

13

Childbearing: Ecstasy or Agony

To the Hebrews, the birth of a child to a family was a mark of divine favor, and thus children were greatly desired (1 Sam. 1:11, 20; Ps. 127:3). This gift of a child prompted unbounded joy, not only for the parents but also for the entire community. On the other hand, the barren womb or the loss of a child by death was the severest of tragedies and a sign of reproach (Gen. 15:2; 30:1; 2 Sam. 6:23; Jer. 22:30; Luke 1:7).

What does the Bible say to contemporary women concerning the question of childbearing? Is it optional or mandatory? Is it a blessing or a curse?

The Edenic Plan

In Genesis 1:28 the Lord commanded the first husband and wife to "multiply, fill the earth" as one of His assigned responsibilities to them and as part of His blessing upon them. When a woman chooses to marry, she assumes the responsibility of being a helper to her husband (Gen. 2:18) and accepts, together with her husband, the opportunity for joining hands with God in the act of creation—bringing new life into existence.

Procreation, however, is not the sole object of marriage, the be-all and end-all of marital bliss. According to God's clear principle of marriage, the union of husband and wife as one flesh (one single being) in itself is complete fulfillment of the divine plan for marriage (Gen. 2:24; see also Matt 19:4–6; Mark 10:5–9; Eph. 5:31). Perfect intimacy and abundant joy marked the relationship between Elkanah and his barren wife Hannah. Upon seeing Hannah's despair and grief, Elkanah reminded his wife, "Am I not better to thee than ten sons?" (1 Sam. 1:18). Through the pen of the apostle Paul, God has given a reminder that you are "to be content in whatever circumstances" you find yourself (Phil. 4:11). If God chooses to allow a womb to remain closed, He has promised to bring joy and happiness into the lives of that couple in other ways.

God has used and will continue to use childless couples to carry out difficult and awesome tasks in His kingdom, for which they would not have been available if they had parenting responsibilities with their own children. Note the prophetess Anna in Luke 2:36–38. She was the first woman to proclaim the good news of God's redemption for Israel. All through the years of her widowhood, she had no child to nurture, but she was busy about kingdom business. No children are mentioned for the dynamic duo Priscilla and Aquila; yet God gave them a unique ministry to many "children in the

Lord." On the other hand, when husband and wife choose to reject the responsibility of parenthood, they stand in violation of a heavenly mandate and need to consider prayerfully their reasons with genuine care and concern. The apostle Paul penned these words: "Therefore, I want younger women to marry, have children, manage their households" (1 Tim. 5:14).

Liabilities in Childbearing

Some stand against procreation as a responsibility in this age because of the population explosion throughout the world. They would look upon this command in a "cultural context" and appropriate the mandate as addressing then but not now.

Of course, there are areas of the world with more people than a country can feed and shelter. Unfortunately, these same countries are without Christian heritage; so Christianity is rapidly becoming the religion of a minority. Even the United States of America, a country established upon a belief and trust in God, every year reveals statistics that are more and more alarming. The number of Christians shrinks proportionately to the growth in population. Many less-developed, pagan countries maintain high rates of growth because of lowered death rates and relatively high, constant birthrates. Developed countries, including the United States, however, have been generally characterized by declining birthrates and aging population. Some of these countries actually have had more deaths than births. According to a report released in October 2012, the "overall fertility rate for women in the U.S.—defined as the number of newborns per 1,000 women aged 15 to 44—was 63.2 last year, down from 64.1 in 2010 and the lowest rate since the government started collecting these statistics in 1920."[1]

The responsibility of parenthood is demanding. The time to count the cost is *before* marriage, since children are a natural, God-given fruit of the loving intimacy between husband and wife. Children do cost money—lots of it. However, couples who choose to remain childless for financial reasons usually find other ways to spend their money. In fact, they often have far more income because the wife can pursue her own career without the responsibility or expense of child care. The entrance of children into a family means changes and sacrifices far beyond financial ones. The couple loses much of its privacy; there are often radical changes in their entire lifestyle. Children can usher in disappointments and sorrows, too.

Considerable pain and suffering are associated with childbirth. In fact, a mother often walks through the valley of the shadow of death in giving birth to a child. Rachel died in giving birth to Benjamin, who later became the father of one of the twelve tribes of Israel. Pain and death in childbirth are the result of sin's presence in the world. The entrance of sin delivered a curse, even upon the blessed act of creating life, by the introduction of pain and suffering to that precious experience (Gen. 3:16).

Rewards in Childbearing

[3]Sons are indeed a heritage from the LORD,
children, a reward.
[4]Like arrows in the hand of a warrior
are the sons born in one's youth.
[5]Happy is the man who has filled his quiver with them.
Such men will never be put to shame

when they speak with their enemies at the city gate.
(Ps. 127:3–5)[2]

There is no higher happiness and joy than that of creating and nurturing life. The simple trust, the tender affection, and the contagious laughter, the mirror of oneself—these are natural qualities of a child.

One can find no deeper pride and sense of fulfillment than that of a father and mother for their offspring. Surely Eunice had tremendous satisfaction in knowing that the apostle Paul had confidence in young Timothy because of the faith she had given her son. Decades ago I accompanied our nine-year-old son on his first missionary journey. What pride and gratitude I felt in my heart as I listened to my son Armour share his testimony in a London classroom.

Children are not only an avenue for service (i.e., an opportunity for providing food and shelter), but they also can reciprocate with comfort and care. I remember a difficult recovery period after surgery on my right hand. My young daughter, who was then only four years old, helped me dress, prepared simple meals under my direction, and even cleaned the house. Although I am not yet so old as to be helpless, my children already minister to my physical needs.

Certainly the spiritual benefits of joining the divine Creator in bringing forth life and molding that life into godly young adulthood cannot be underestimated. What other pursuit in all the world offers as much opportunity for creativity (Ps. 139:14–16) or demands as much in skills and energies?

Susannah Wesley had many children, among them John and Charles Wesley. She poured herself into the lives of her children, giving them her best, and surely she must have looked down from the glory of her heavenly home with infinite pride in her offspring and a profound satisfaction over their contribution to the kingdom of Christ.

My own mother is talented and capable. As my father's full business partner, she has proven her abilities to handle administrative and financial responsibilities with expertise and finesse. Yet, if one were to compare her value to the business world with her contribution as a mother, the comparison would be ludicrous. As a devoted, full-time mother, she reared a preacher son, wives for two preachers, a nurse, and one elementary schoolteacher. Her son and her son-in-love (my husband) are now presidents of seminaries. My sisters and I also take delight in our service to the Lord. Could our mother have done anything else more profitable for the kingdom of Christ or even more beneficial to the world? Had she determined to put aside the responsibility of childbearing, perhaps the world would be poorer still for lack of the five she reared to honor and serve the Lord.

"But she will be saved through childbearing, if she continues in faith, love, and holiness, with good judgment" (1 Tim. 2:15). This verse is a reference to the calling of a woman to be a wife and mother as her primary role in life. The anxieties, pains, and dangers accompanying maternity are the results of sin. The woman is not saved by childbearing instrumentally as a means of salvation but positionally as faithful keeper of her assigned sphere as wife and mother. What *greater* influence and usefulness can a woman achieve than molding the next generation?

You have only to look at the statistics of the world religions to understand the Edenic command from *Yahweh* (God) to repopulate the world, followed by the emphasis to rear up the following generation in the nurture and honor of the Lord (Deut. 6:4–9). Godly parenting is a primary means of evangelization (i.e., passing the good news of the gospel from generation to generation). To continue the race and raise up a Christian generation demands responsible Christian parents who gladly accept the mandate of heaven to give life and training to their children, who will be the next generation. To continue the propagation of God's Word and to be His ambassadors and evangelists, you and I must simply rear up a generation for the Lord (Ps. 78:1–8).

Conclusion

How do husband and wife resolve this difficult dilemma? First, they must seek the Lord's face, laying before Him their reasons for choosing to avoid the responsibility of parent-hood. Then, they must decide: Are these God-inspired rea-sons, or are they human conjecture based upon convenience and worldly values? Children are a most precious gift from the Lord. Nothing is as demanding and time-consuming or as rewarding as the rearing of these little ones unto the Lord. Nothing in this world I have ever done—the writing of books, the broadcasting assignments on radio and television, the delivering of messages, the teaching of classes, or travel-ing across the world—equals the joy and satisfaction I have personally experienced in molding the lives of my children. According to Scripture, the opportunity for parenthood is divinely given and not to be taken lightly or to be cast aside based on human whims. Only God Himself, in His own providence and omniscience, reserves the right to determine whether the womb is to remain barren. If God wills, I pray for every wife the privilege of bearing a child!

Notes

1. Conor Dougherty, "U.S. Fertility Rate Hits Lowest Level on Record," WSJ Blogs (*Wall Street Journal*), October 3, 2012 [online]; accessed October 4, 2012; available from http://blogs.wsj.com/economics/2012/10/03/u-s-fertility-rate-hits-lowest-level-on-record/. The article refers to a report released by the Centers for Disease Control and Prevention (CDC) of the U.S. Department of Health and Human Services: Brady E. Hamilton, Joyce A. Martin, and Stephanie J. Ventura, "Births: Preliminary Data for 2011," *National Vital Statistics Reports* 61.5 (October 3, 2012).

2. See Amanda Walker's application of this passage in her blog entry for *BiblicalWoman.org*: "Are Your Kids Ready to Launch?" (August 23, 2012); available at http://www.biblicalwoman.org/voices/index.php/category/relationships/parenting-relationships. Also see at this web site Dorothy Kelley Patterson's column answering the question, "Dear Dottie: Should I Hold Off on Having Children?" (February 5, 2013); available from http://www.biblicalwoman.org/voices/index.php/2013/02/05/dear-dottie-should-i-hold-off-on-having-children.

14

A Word to Children: Stretch Your Minds and Build Your Faith

The end of summer is a dreaded time for many children and young people. The months of freedom and play are gone again, and students must return to the discipline and regimentation of the academic world. How does a child or young person prepare for a new school year, or is there any need for preparation? What are the ingredients that make happy productivity for the average youth?

A Spiritual Commitment

There is no more important task for beginning anew than establishing or refueling your commitment to Jesus Christ. The young person who is related personally to Jesus Christ must regularly renew that commitment with heart and life. There is no time in life when the personal quiet time for reading the Scriptures and praying is more needed, pouring out your heart and soul before the Father, asking for protection from the evil one who walks about seeking to devour the young and inexperienced (Prov. 1:8–19; 4:10–27), petitioning the Father for physical needs, and seeking wisdom for difficult days.

In addition to the necessity of regular spiritual sustenance, there is the need for ministry to others, using your God-given talents and divinely bestowed spiritual gifts. Service to Christ is never relegated to later years but is demanded throughout all your years. My son went on his first missionary journey at age nine, sharing his testimony in schools, churches, and with individuals. There is no more opportune time for witnessing than during the formative years before individuals become hardened against the gospel.

An Intellectual Challenge

The years of academic preparation should be a time of stretching the mind and developing a discipline for study (Eccles. 12:12; 2 Tim. 2:15). Good study habits will be as helpful in your child's career as any acquired knowledge. The mind is an intricate mechanism designed to blend together the storage of knowledge, the distribution of action, and the motivation of attitude. There is a *price* to be paid in learning, but there is also a *prize* to be won in achieving. The wise Solomon admonished the youth again and again, knowing the untapped and unpolluted potential found in a young life (Eccles. 12:1). Make this a year in which you "redeem the time," attacking your studies and assignments with vigor and purpose.

A Social Climate

There is never a more opportune time for making friend-ships than in the days of youth when peers are so much a part of life. The Scriptures have much to say about friendships. The most significant guideline is to be "in" the world, loving and ministering, but not "of" the world. We are admonished not to be "unequally yoked" (NKJV) or joined with an unbe-liever (2 Cor. 6:14). These words are not merely a prohibition for marriage between a believer and nonbeliever, but they are also a warning about any serious relationship with a non-believer. Christians need the fellowship and encouragement of those who are like-minded (Amos 3:3). These are days of forming lifelong friendships, but young people must be encouraged to choose those friends according to the guide-lines given in Scripture.

An Emotional Climb

The years of preparation are plagued with more pressures, not only in the classroom, where there is much competition and some confusion, but also in extracurricular activities. Girls sometimes find themselves left out of clubs and unin-vited to parties because of intrigue and selfish designs. I have watched young boys sit faithfully on the bench during the rookie year because the older boys were better, and then I have seen older boys denied starting status and kept on the bench just because the coach was down on them. There are classroom teachers who hate children and react with hostility to normal activities of childhood. In the divine economy, however, even the most tragic happenings will be turned into good lessons in life for those who love the Lord and are His children (see Rom. 8:28). Spiritual rearing and maturing are moved along by the difficulties you face and the mountains you climb.

Epilogue to Children

Every child and young person should be encouraged to line up under the authorities God has placed in their lives—parents in the home, teachers in the school, employer in work, and pastor in church (see Eph. 6:4; Heb. 13:7). In addition to obedience to earthly authorities, you should submit to the Lord in a daily time of reading Scripture and praying as a means of preparing yourself for battle with Satan (see Matt. 6:33; Eph. 6:10–20). Finally, do your dead-level best in studies, athletics, and every activity—"as to the Lord" (Eph. 5:22).

15

Entering the World of Your Teenager

Some occupations have built-in hazards—window washers on buildings that reach to the sky, F-16 pilots in a shooting war, news correspondents in Lebanon, *and* mothers! Motherhood never appeared so hazardous and life-threatening to me until my only son entered the modern-day gladiatorial combat commonly called football. That was three decades ago, and the athletic challenges have only multiplied to more choices in sports and to include daughters as well as sons in the field sports! According to my friend Betsy Owens, the concussion rate for female college soccer players is two-and-a-half times the rate for male football players.

My husband assured me that there were no dangers for our son as we rushed out to buy a thickly padded helmet with its own air pump, which must be used from time to time to re-inflate the lining of the helmet after its weekly battering. The school furnished pads for shoulders, thighs, hips, and knees, and we could and did pick up extras for neck, arms, and hands. In addition, those who wanted to be especially careful wrapped with tape all other visible body parts. Yet, the game is not dangerous, they claim; all this paraphernalia and preparation is merely part of its mystique!

What Do You Wear?

During my son's athletic pursuits, you could always spot a football player's mom. She was perfectly coordinated, or at least reasonably attired in the school colors, which often necessitated her wearing the same outfit to all the games. By the end of the season you could identify her from a distance—by clothes instead of facial features! My fashion image suffered further from the necessity of centering my wardrobe around the special collector's T-shirt with my son's name and number. Of course, manufacturing such an item was a mixture of Russian roulette and "spendthrift-itis" because of the musical-shirt game. The afternoon your shirt was imprinted your son's number was changed! Added to team colors and brag shirts were the numerous buttons and ribbons—a weekly ribbon identifying the opponent, a picture button identifying your son, and the Booster Club button announcing your "professional" affiliation. In addition, I was *fortunate* enough to have a Booster Club hat as well. I understand that most of these accoutrements are now obsolete, but I do run into huge traveling groups descending on economy hotels throughout the country as family and friends follow their own respective athletes. Their gear is more centered around ice chests and bags of snacks than specialized clothing and accessories.

What Do You Take with You? *

When our son's football career began, he spent the first season learning how to wear his jersey, how to stand expectantly and confidently on the sidelines, how to drink from the water bottles on the run with optimum peripheral vision. This gave me time to develop my own entertainment in order to fill idle hours and calm frayed nerves between my son's trips on and off the field.

Needlepoint was my option, since I did it with only one stitch and the process needed no concentration! In this era moms may opt for answering e-mails or playing games on their electronic devices. Along the way you will also acquire a stadium seat (it helps your failing fashion image to color coordinate this with your team colors); binoculars (this makes you look more professional); your own coffee or tea in a thermos; your own snacks (you may miss his greatest play of the season, or worse still, his *only* play, if you have to leave the stands); your rain gear (this helps to postpone the downpour, which only comes when you have no umbrella or rain hat or even a paper sack to cover your head). As I became more experienced, I learned that for all teams except the varsity, at least one foraging mom had to nag the coaches until a roster was produced. I made points with fellow football moms by typing up names and numbers and making copies for everyone.

What Can You Do for Your Son? *

Encourage Him

Participation in sporting events is marked with ups and downs. One year our son would be in all his glory and never leave the field—an upperclassman and an experienced player. The next year no one even knew what position he would play, and he went back to warming the bench or acting as meat for the varsity lions. Here you can shine, for no one can encourage and praise like a mother! The writer of Proverbs said, "Anxiety in a man's heart weighs it down, but a good word cheers it up" (12:25), and ". . . a timely word—how good that is!" (15:23).

Look for the good in your child's performance and offer sincere praise. Do not deny the bad, but emphasize the lessons learned from mistakes (see Prov. 13:18). Of course, you cannot encourage effectively unless you are there to see him. He may spend more time on the field warming up than he logs in playing time during the game. If so, do not miss the pregame warm-up! A child's self-esteem can suffer terrific blows from yelling coaches and jeering fans, but a mother can lovingly and creatively remind him of his worth and encourage him never to give up (Prov. 23:7; 25:11). A boy's suffering may become God's school (Prov. 24:10) with your gentle and persistent guidance.

Build His Faith

Teach your son to look to God for strength to do his best and for comfort in time of hurts (Isa. 43:2). Remind him that God is ultimately the giver of a strong body and athletic skills.

Remind your son to thank his Creator for these gifts (James 1:17).

Develop His Character Qualities

What better way is there to learn patient endurance than on a muddy football field with the score stacked against you and a deep heart's desire to win? (Heb. 12:1–2). Where is a better test of humility than to sit on the sideline never having had a fair chance to show your skills? (Rom. 12:3; James 4:10). How can you learn obedience without question any more quickly than to be given an assignment that you think is unfair or wrong or fruitless? (Heb. 13:17). Is there any faster road to a disciplined lifestyle than demanding maximum strength and performance from your body and learning that this means daily exercise, a consistent nutritional diet, and adequate rest, followed by pushing each member of your body to do its best? (Eccles. 9:10; 12:1). How can he better learn cooperation as part of a team effort where he must put the good of the team before his own personal desires? (Eccles. 4:9–10).

Minister to His Spirit

This privilege is open to you during these brief years. For example, during the rugged, life-threatening, spirit-crushing "two-a-days" characteristic of preparation for the football season, you can accept the extra chauffeuring (four trips daily) with joy and be prompt, even if it means sitting in a hot car when the boys are running late. You can creatively look for ways to make it easier. I bought a large water bottle and twice daily filled it with ice and water so my son could be refreshed with that "cup of cold water." You can do a quick washing of the perspiration-soaked clothes in the middle of the day and/ or the evening as is needed. You can be part of the parent-support groups working for the team's financial needs. You can be sensitive to "a broken spirit" (Prov. 18:14) and ready to listen and encourage.

This, Too, Shall Pass!

This word is my final and best counsel. When your child is bruised and battered, when his spirit is wounded and broken, when he is discouraged and hurt, when you think you cannot sit through another demoralizing defeat, remember the words of the wise Solomon: "The end of a matter is better than its beginning; a patient spirit is better than a proud spirit (Eccles. 7:8).

Note

* These same principles I used with my football-playing son would work with a daughter pursuing athletics.

16

The Hearth of Home: Build the Fire and Stoke the Flame

The dictionary defines the family as "the body of persons who live in one house, under one head" or "the group formed by parents and children." This definition is rapidly becoming obsolete as Satan continues his vicious onslaught against the Lord's first institution. Satan is aware that the home is precious to the Lord and valuable to His kingdom's work. Through the home, spiritual truths are best taught, and the joining together of families forms the church and undergirds its work.

The Distortion of God's Plan for the Home

In the garden of Eden, the Lord Himself made the man and gave him the authority to oversee the garden paradise.

Then, the divine plan added a helper for the man—a woman to assist Him in the responsibilities of the garden and to have fellowship with Him (see Gen. 2:15–17). When Satan tempted the pristine couple, causing them to sin and to break their fellowship with the Creator, God did not give up His plan for the home, nor did He revise that plan. However, Satan has changed his method of attack again and again in an effort to destroy the home and its spiritual ministry through causing difficult and trying circumstances, through manipulating selfish and carnal people, and through continually questioning the Word of God.

The entrance of sin into the world has made keeping a clear biblical pattern for the home extremely difficult. Husbands have abandoned the headship assigned by God Himself, and wives have rebelled against the leadership of their husbands so that "the body of persons who live in one house" are no longer "under one head" (see Gen. 3:1). In fact, *Merriam Webster's* latest definition of "family" reads "the body of persons . . . usually under one head."[1] Instead of parents and children binding themselves into one unity, each family member does "his own thing" and goes his own way.

God's Plan for the Home

First God established a "garden" (a shelter or haven; see Gen. 2:8). Every family unit needs a place prepared and equipped to meet the needs of each individual. There must be the security of love, the loyalty of protecting, the fellowship of communication, and the nurture of spiritual training. God named the garden paradise "Eden," meaning "delight."

Every home should be "Eden," a place of delight, joy, and

comfort to those in the family circle and to those whom God would send to the home for ministry. Many conveniences and work-saving devices are available to the home in the modern era, but someone has to care enough to assume primary responsibility for organizing and overseeing the household (see 1 Tim. 5:14).

My husband and I are privileged to be in many churches across the nation. One of our favorites is Rock Springs Baptist Church in Easley, South Carolina. On a Sunday after the pastor's wife, Shirley Gallamore, had done the special music with the Gallamore Trio in both services, she invited us to their home for lunch. What an oasis of orderliness with the aroma of culinary delicacies wafting through the air as we walked through the door after Sunday morning worship and made our way almost immediately through a buffet presenting the *menu du jour* of simple but beautifully presented food and then gathered around a table of fellowship for what was a meaningful climax to a Lord's Day morning. We filled our stomachs and our hearts and then left as quickly as we arrived to make our way back to our lodging for a brief rest before the evening service. That evening Shirley again was in her place in the choir. I was blessed and inspired to see in action a pastor's wife who is truly a helper in ministry and yet also such an efficient manager of her household that she could care for her family's mundane needs at the table as well as welcome and minister to us. I can guarantee that no one has had a bigger part in the effectiveness of this pastor's ministry than his devoted and talented wife with God-given priorities. Your menu may be as simple as pancakes, which were my entrée for guests when we were in seminary. I gathered recipes and experimented until I was prepared to adapt them to any meal accompanied by a simple green salad for dinner or fruit salad for brunch. The important thing is loving and serving those whom God brings to your home.

After preparation of the "home" in the garden, God placed in its midst the man, whom He created in His own image, and assigned to that man responsibility for overseeing the work of the garden. He could have made the man self-sufficient, but God created him with a physical, social, and emotional need for a helpmate. After establishing the man's authority and headship by primacy of creation and divine assignments as recorded in Scripture, God then made the woman. He showed His plan and purpose for the couple again in the method of creation by taking a part of the man, rather than another handful of dirt, to make the woman. Husband and wife were united in marriage by God Himself with an explicit directive that their union was to be monogamous, intimate, and permanent (see Gen. 2:18, 24).

From the beginning, the first couple were instructed to join with the Creator in bringing life into the world and rearing up a generation unto the Lord (Gen. 1:28). The responsibility of parenthood is not optional or negotiable. The Lord has made clear throughout Scripture that children are a gift from God, literally "a heritage from the Lord" and "a reward" (see Ps. 127:3). God does not give to husband and wife a greater and more important responsibility than that of parenthood. The challenge of nurturing a child in the Lord and rearing him to walk in the path of righteousness is an awesome opportunity to pass the teachings of *Yahweh* God to the next generation.

What Does the Home Do for the Kingdom?

Families join together to make up churches. Just as blood is the lifeline of the body, even so Christian families are the essence of the church and the embodiment of its programs. The church does not have the complete responsibility for the spiritual nurture and the teaching of Scripture and its truths.

The home is still God's *primary* teaching tool because in its very design are found pictures of your relationship to the heavenly Father and clear illustrations of spiritual truths. God's blessing is upon the home because He has a task for the home to perform in the kingdom. My husband and I, as well as our extended family, pray that Christian families across our land might join their hands and hearts with ours so we can "proclaim Yahweh's greatness . . . [and] exalt His name together" (Ps. 34:3).

Notes

1. The word "family," *Merriam-Webster.com*, http://www.merriam-webster.com (8 February 2013).

17

Grandparents: Enriching the Next Generation

Noah was a righteous man, blameless among his contemporaries; Noah walked with God. (Gen. 6:9)

Faith in God

One of the most precious responsibilities of grandparents is the sharing of their faith from generation to generation. Noah's righteousness was certainly inspired and nurtured by his ancestors (Gen. 5:22–25, 28–29), and this unusual spiritual heritage uniquely equipped him to withstand the onslaught of ungodly and wicked contemporaries.

A special bond often exists between grandparents and

grandchildren—a bond of love and affection that opens communication in a unique and penetrating manner. Grandparents are honored for their years of wisdom and needed for their loving sensitivity. They have the privilege of reinforcing the godly lessons taught by parents and supplementing the spiritual nurture of the younger generation. Note the example of the godly grandmother Lois, who actively participated in the spiritual training of her grandson Timothy:

> . . . that I may be filled with joy, clearly recalling your
> sincere faith that first lived in your grandmother Lois,
> then in your mother Eunice, and that I am convinced
> is in you also. (2 Tim. 1:4–5)

The patriarchal couple Francis and Edith Schaeffer have left an impressive legacy to the Christian world in books, tapes, films, and so forth, but surpassing all of these is the uniquely inspiring testimony of their life and ministry together—the Schaeffer family, issuing forth generation after generation who honor the Lord and who love one another.

Memories of the Past

Grandparents are a living memory album, an interesting collage of the past, an open book of history. Children often look to grandparents as a continuity with the past. How delightful to hear firsthand experiences of years gone by, which are now written in history books. The past is a valuable tool with which to build for the future. Our son Armour gave us a photograph from a time we enjoyed at the Southern Baptist Convention in Utah—a special memory when his father was elected president. He attached this meaningful verse: "Listen to Me . . . : Look to the rock *from which* you were hewn" (Isa. 51:1 NKJV).

The Lord frequently reminded Israel of those who had gone before—Abraham, Isaac, Jacob (Gen. 28:13; Exod. 6:2–3). Even this generation responds with interest and attentiveness to the past. One of the most popular television programs for my children in their younger years was *The Waltons*, a series based on the true experiences of a mountain family spanning four generations. The program not only supplied information and satisfied curiosities concerning the past but also touched the heart and reached to the soul with its presentation of the trials common to the human family, accompanied by ways in which difficulties were lovingly resolved or weathered by the resources of the extended family.

Security

Grandparents who have withstood the ravages of time are often held in awe and reverence by the younger generation. This is especially true in Asian families where respect for age is taught and expected. The one who reaches old age is honored for this wisdom and rewarded for perseverance. Note, for example, the Old Testament patriarchs listed in the "Roll Call of the Faithful" (Heb. 11). Age is certainly one of the tests of faith. The fact that you have received a word from God and acted in obedience to the divine command again and again through the years leaves a dynamic and vital testimony for those to come.

One such patriarch who touched my own life was a godly pastor we affectionately called Preacher Hallock. I first met him during my husband's pastorate in Fayetteville, Arkansas.

I can still remember his sharing the precious truths of God's Word, especially concerning prayer and the promises of God. Some years later I met his missionary son, and then I heard a missionary message from his preacher grandson, who told me about the birth of his own child. Preacher Hallock went to be with the Lord years ago, but who can know, save our Lord Himself, how many godly generations will arise from this legacy?

Enrichment

Grandparents often do or give beyond that which parents are able to do or give. "Your two sons born to you in the land of Egypt before I came to you in Egypt are now mine. Ephraim and Manasseh belong to me" (Gen. 48:5). Joseph had gone through many hardships and difficulties, having survived sibling rejection, lengthy imprisonment, and even attempts upon his life. His children were born in a pagan land, cut off from kindred and spiritual blessing, but God worked through the grandfather Jacob to overcome obstacles and to give his grandsons more than their father could offer.

Enrichment is not limited to that which can be purchased with money. My children's paternal grandmother has given them a unique heritage in writing a collection of short stories featuring her grandchildren, their parents, and various members of the extended family, as well as imaginary pets who become heroic adventurers. She painted portraits of the pets and even purchased inexpensive stuffed facsimiles of the animals. Carmen and Armour will have a permanent reminder of their grandmother through the unique "Fodsdick and Tertullian Stories."

The In-between Generation

Parents, too, are recipients of the benefits of grandparenting. They have access to counsel based upon the years of knowledge and experience already banked in these human computers. They receive cooperation and encouragement as they feel the awesome demands of parenthood, and they can find some coaching and tutoring available for the asking. Furthermore, parents can turn to grandparents even for rest!

What Do the Grandparents Get Out of All This?

Children's children *are* the crown of old men. (Prov. 17:6 NKJV)

The rewards available to grandparents are many and varied. No laughter and joy inspires like that of a child. Every visit from the grandchildren leaves a volume of anecdotes and humorous stories. There is a unique dimension to the comfort of a child and an added zest to the tender care of one who is gentle in manner and unspoiled by the busyness of the world. There is pride in seeing your own mark on another generation, the touch of your influence even from afar.

Epilogue

A good man leaves an inheritance to his grandchildren, but the sinner's wealth is stored up for the righteous. (Prov. 13:22)

Every family is an artwork, as Edith Schaeffer suggests, and has already passed the test of antiquity—our families are genuine antiques. We all have roots, though they may be disguised and hidden. The artwork of a family is continued generation after generation. It takes time to become a grandparent—at least three generations must appear through those many years of sickness and health, poverty and wealth, death and birth, ups and downs, trials and joys, tears and laughter.

Grandparents, lend your ears! Have you a faith to pass on? Will you plan time to share that faith and teach those spiritual truths?

During his childhood, my son's room was marked by a collection of photos, including his great-grandfather, his grandfather, his father, two of his uncles, and a cousin—all preachers. These beloved men of faith are his forefathers, and I wanted to keep them before him as examples. My daughter had a similar collection of photos of the women in her family—great-grandmother, grandmothers, mother, and aunts. This treasury of memories reminds her of the heritage God has given her.

Grandparents should always leave a legacy to grandchildren—a personal possession, such as a worn Bible with special notes; a poem or storybook; a financial gift for education; a handmade article. Security is largely measured by ways of saying "we care about you." My husband and I were helped through some lean and difficult years by a small monthly check from the estate of his grandparents. My grandmother gave her priceless works of textile art, fashioned by her own hands, to us and to our children.

Grandparents can contribute the most lasting gift, however, by giving of themselves during a child's lifetime. Our children's maternal grandparents bestowed their undivided attention on them in planning and executing happy experiences—a fishing trip, a special movie, a ride in Papa's plane or boat, homemade goodies to eat, special cards and letters throughout the year, and continued personal interest in what they are doing. Give enrichment to your grandchildren, sharing your knowledge and introducing them to new experiences. Lady Bird Johnson, wife of the late President Lyndon Baines Johnson, was once asked why she did not accept a government position worthy of her skills and experience. She replied firmly, "I would rather be near my children and grandchildren." Read her biographies to confirm that she took that commitment seriously.

In the family, you do not work yourself out of a job with age; you simply extend and adapt your responsibilities. Parenting is a lifetime pursuit, but it becomes "grander" still when extended over the generations. If the grandparents of the world could be called back to active duty, wouldn't it make a difference in the next generation?

18

Family Mealtime: Food for the Body and Encouragement for the Soul

These all wait for You,
That You may give *them* their food in due season.
(Ps. 104:27 NKJV)

The context for this verse is an ode of praise to the God of creation—God who gives and sustains life and bestows blessings and favor upon His creation.

Responsibilities

The home is God's first institution, and the one who keeps that home has considerable responsibility to the heavenly Father. Hopefully, a desire will awaken in the hearts of homemakers today to find new excitement in planning and preparation for the family mealtime.

In the modern era, few people experience the joy and relaxation of having food in due season. Many families eat in shifts, often with each family member—including children—responsible for planning and preparing his own meal. The mass exodus of women from the home, the belittling of homemaking responsibilities, the appeal of convenience foods, the lure of adventuresome restaurants, the breakdown in family communication, the rapid advance of electronic social media to replace personal interaction, the acceleration of individual pursuits within the family circle—all of these factors have contributed to the elimination of family time, even the brief meal around the table.

Benefits

First and foremost in the benefits of mealtime is the nourishment of the body. Nutrition is a vital science that offers to the astute homemaker information in meal planning. Actually, food preparation itself is only a minor part of the total responsibility of feeding the family. Meals should be planned daily, by the week, or even by the month, with attention given to a balanced diet as well as to how the food is served. Amazingly food tastes much better when arranged attractively and artistically on the plate.

Another benefit of the family mealtime is the spirit of fellowship and sharing that ought to be a natural complement of this regular gathering. It provides an opportunity to talk about the day's activities ahead, in process, and those already gone by. Table conversation should be relaxed and happy and should include everyone. This may be the last frontier for family fellowship with the mobility and diversity of the current generation. We Pattersons had to eat in restaurants far more than we would have preferred because, in order to be together, we often found it necessary to go downtown near my husband's office so we could have quality family time in the midst of his responsibilities. We also reinstituted "Sunday Dinner" at our home, including the grandparents, aunts and uncles, and cousins, and often others. Especially was this our pattern when the children were at home and when we lived near members of our extended family. This weekly time with the family is well worth the planning and preparation in order to keep those ties strong.

Family meals can also offer for the children a training ground in manners and etiquette. There is no better way to learn how to behave at the table than from firsthand experience! Occasionally you can have fun setting the table for a formal dinner—service plate, dinner plate, salad plate, bread-and-butter plate, together with extra pieces of flatware—to give the children practice in choosing the correct utensil and working through multi-course meals.

Finally, however, is the spiritual benefit. While feeding your body with vegetables and meat, you must not neglect to feed your soul with the Bread of Life. Mealtime is one of the best opportunities for family worship—prayer, reading Scripture, and sharing mutual spiritual concerns as well as discussing spiritual truths.

19

Family Time: Memorable Fun and Lasting Legacy

The old cliché, "The family that plays or prays together, stays together," is certainly more truth than fiction. Most of the time, getting the family to sleep together under one roof is not a big problem. Until the children's teen years, with any success at all, at least some meals will be shared together. However, the selfish philosophy of recent decades has really eroded the time for family fun and entertainment, and family worship has been all but eliminated.

The Changing Generations

There was a day when the only entertainment available was within the family unit. Without movies, television, or readily available transportation, family members were reduced to their own resources. Indoor and outdoor games called for participation from the entire family. Picnics and outings usually included all the family. The idea of everyone doing his "own thing" and going his own way was seldom considered.

The affluence enjoyed by this generation has been both curse and blessing. You and I have been blessed beyond imagination, being able to provide for our children unprecedented opportunities in education and travel. My husband and I are grateful beyond expression that our children attended a Christian academy with God-honoring curriculum and Christlike teachers. We have been blessed with the privilege of taking our children—and even our grandchildren—throughout the United States and even to many foreign countries so they have seen other cultures, peoples, and customs firsthand.

On the other hand, in some ways this generation has been cursed with the mobility and mechanization that have often cut into its family time. You may be tempted to turn on the television or take the children to a movie or sports arena instead of stretching your minds with word games or going on a picnic or nature hike. The demands of a frantic society in an age of unparalleled busyness has sliced into mealtime, and the introduction of convenience foods and the vast array of public eating facilities have made the move from dwindling private family hours into the rapidly expanding public marketplace easy.

Likewise, from the era of the Old Testament patriarchs to the days of our founding fathers, who were pioneers in a new land of promise, worship was primarily within the family unit. The Scriptures were read and taught within the home (see Deut. 6:4–9). In the modern day, the teaching of doctrine and morality has been shifted to church and school. Many parents even expect the church to provide transportation for their children!

Is There a Word from God?

The psalmist penned these Spirit-breathed words: "God sets the solitary in families" (Ps. 68:6 NKJV). There is no greater need in Christian homes than that time be faithfully allotted and earnestly guarded for the family to be alone in worship and praise to the Creator and in fun and fellowship with one another. God has never wavered from His plan to use the family unit in teaching spiritual truth, in undergirding the work of the kingdom, and in ministering to one another in love and strength.

The Pattersons have committed themselves anew through the years to family loyalties. At breakfast we have worshiped together by using the missionary prayer calendar, with our own added prayer requests, and by reading from the Scriptures together as a family. We have also worked at having time together as a family. Even in our senior years, my husband and I look to summer as a joyous period when we can log more family hours. My husband has always had to travel a great deal, but in the summer Mommy *and* the children could fit our schedule to his and travel with him, and now we find our granddaughters more available in these months. Sometimes cramped quarters and unfamiliar beds, long hours in car or plane, the monotony of meals eaten in bland restaurants, and the inconvenience of living out of a suitcase have infringed upon our dispositions and become times of testing. Nevertheless, we have had hours together to talk and visit. We have had opportunities for playing games and seeing new places. We have met people and made friends, and we have spent lots of quality time with one another.

A Challenge for You and Yours

Is your family a priority? Are your spouse and children important enough for you to schedule regular and uninterrupted times to be with them—and to enjoy and focus upon them with the same commitment you would have in preparing a meal, cleaning a room, or pursuing a career goal? Have you seen the historic sites where you live? Have you taken a trip together? Have you taken a nature hike or visited a local zoo or museum? Have you planned an exclusive family outing? Have you discussed current events with one another? Have you practiced corporate family worship? May God give us Christian homes alive with laughter and fun and secure in relaxation and contentment!

20

Widowhood: Fertile Field or Desolate Desert

As the daughter of a funeral director and the wife of a preacher, I have been around death all of my life. Although death produces sorrow and a vacuum every time it strikes, I believe there is no greater heartache than losing your spouse. The separation of two who have joined themselves together as one in life and purpose is both difficult and traumatic. Often sharing a burden with each other is replaced with struggling in self-pity by the one alone; the fun of fellowship together is changed to the fear of loneliness on the part of the one left; the delight of common ministry shared as a couple is pushed aside by the surviving spouse through the despondency of withdrawal from every task of service.

A "widow" is a woman who has outlived her husband. What is the place of the widow in today's world? What are the options open to her? In the Old Testament, the Hebrew word translated "widow" is 'almanah, literally the "silent one," and in the New Testament the Greek word is chēra, literally the "bereft one."

The words themselves are expressive. You can examine the message of the words in a negative light and presume that the widow is "silent," overwhelmed by the power of the grave and death; or you can review the widow's silence positively as a refusal to argue with God over her untimely sorrow, not as a resignation to cruel fate but as a resting in gracious, divine providence.

The latter viewpoint is surely harmonious with the apostle Peter's directive to women in which he notes that the "gentle and quiet spirit" is a costly and valuable "ornament" in the sight of God. The widow, then, has the challenge of seeking quietness, stillness, and calmness, which can only come from a confidence in the providence and faithfulness of Yahweh God. Her "resting" in the Lord is in itself a testimony to the goodness of the Lord as El Shaddai, the Almighty, the self-sufficient and all-sufficient Ruler of all. Furthermore, the widow by her "silence" is free to listen to God and to develop profound sensitivity to His leadership. Instead of considering herself "bereft" of provider and protector or robbed of husband and friend, the widow can determine with gratitude that God's confidence in her is great enough to entrust her with a difficult assignment and to give her opportunity for meaningful testimony (Jer. 49:11). She also has a matchless opportunity to develop her faith and trust in the Lord.

When a woman loses her husband (the one divinely assigned to protect and provide for her; cp. Gen. 2:15–17),

God Himself then makes a personal commitment to protect her (Deut. 14:28–29; 24:17–21; Jer. 22:3; Zech. 7:10). It is a comforting, beautiful assurance to know that an omnipresent, omnipotent, omniscient God is watching tenderly over the widow, providing for her physical needs (Deut. 10:18), guarding against dangers to her (Ps. 121:1–8, a special word of encouragement to the widow), and faithfully directing her life (cp. Prov. 3:5–6; 1 Cor. 10:13). The Lord furthermore will bring judgment and punishment upon any who wrong the widow (Exod. 22:22–24; Mal. 3:5; Matt. 23:14).

"The Lord destroys the house of the proud, but He protects the widow's territory" (Prov. 15:25). This verse is an awesome testimony to the responsibility the Lord accepts concerning the widow. He promises to "protect" (establish, make sure) her "territory." There is the connotation of remaining or standing firm, permanent and immovable. "Territory" refers to a border or boundary (a landmark or an enclosed place; cp. Deut. 19:14). In other words, God seems to place an invisible wall around the widow. But how can a widow secure this divine protection and special blessing? God does not force Himself or His beneficence on anyone. So, the widow who wants His protective care must consecrate or set herself apart to the Lord. Through her own faith and commitment she steps into and remains within the boundaries of God's protective area.

First, then, a widow must consecrate herself to the Lord, accept her position in Him (Phil. 4:11), and determine to follow the Lord's leadership in her life and ministry (Phil. 4:13). This commitment to the Lord moves her from vulnerability to Satan's favorite tools of assault against widows—self-pity, idleness, uselessness, and despair (1 Tim. 5:13) and opens her to a new assignment from God in ministry and service.

In the book of Ruth, Naomi falls prey to Satan's attack and allows her life to be immersed in self-pity and bitterness (1:20–21). What a beautiful change comes in her heart when she trusts herself to Boaz, the kinsman-redeemer (Hebrew, *go'ēl*), who not only provides her physical necessities (2:15–18) but also restores her life when Obed is born to Ruth (4:15–17). For every widow, God is the Kinsman-Redeemer who not only wants to meet her physical needs but also desires to restore life and joy (Job 29:13).

What are some special ministries for the widow?

- *Prayer*—Anna was continually in God's house, and her life was characterized by godliness because of the many hours she spent in prayer and fasting. Surely there are no more effective prayer warriors in the world than godly widows who devote countless hours to communication with God (cp. Luke 2:36–38).

- *Counsel*—Naomi, after her cleansing of heart and renewal of purpose, was a marvelous counselor to Ruth. The wise widow shared meaningful insights with Ruth (cp. Ruth 1–4). Counsel may be enhanced by teaching, and God gives a clear directive to the older or the spiritually mature women, charging them to teach the younger women (Titus 2:3–5). Often the widow is equipped by both experience and wisdom for this task.

- *Service*—The younger widow, Ruth, was God's instrument for redeeming Naomi from a life of self-pity to usefulness, for restoring the lonely Boaz to joy, and for giving life to Obed, an ancestor of the promised Messiah. Ruth's optimism in the most difficult of circumstances and cheerful diligence to even the most menial tasks were a sweet fragrance to Boaz and a meaningful testimony to the providence of God.

- *Hospitality*—The unnamed widow of Zarephath extended gracious hospitality to Elijah (1 Kings 17:8–24). By opening her home to those who are weary and hurting, a widow can satisfy her heartfelt hunger for human companionship and fellowship (cp. 1 Tim. 5:10).

- *Giving*—There is no more poignant testimony of stewardship in all Scripture than the widow who gave all she had to the Lord (Mark 12:41–44; Luke 21:1–4). Because of her humble and uncertain circumstances, the widow's giving is especially touching to the Lord.

- *Faith*—The widow with the pot of oil faced an intolerable situation—being bereft of her husband in the prime of life, having heavy indebtedness, losing her sons to slavery; however, she followed the divine guidelines and sought counsel from a man of God and obeyed that counsel in faith (2 Kings 4:17). God blessed her faith, and she honored and glorified the Lord (Ps. 146:8).

When God unites a man and a woman in marriage, He does so to enable them to do together what neither could do alone (Ps. 34:3). On the other hand, when the Lord takes one partner to be with Him in the heavenly home, He restores the one left on earth and gives to her a new assignment to ministry and a fresh opportunity for spiritual growth.

21

Creative Hospitality: Sharing What You Have through Who You Are

Never have I been more overwhelmed with creativity and hospitality than during my visit to the Central Baptist Church in Aurora, Colorado. This dynamic fellowship of believers, who have had as pastor several of our "children" in the ministry, is marked by gifted and gracious women. They invited me to speak to their women at a Saturday evening banquet and in additional gatherings on Sunday. I was there to minister to and edify them. However, I received a delightful surprise.

Already I had delivered a series of messages to a Denver retreat. I was tired and a bit weary. My Aurora hostess Laurie Sellers picked me up at my second hotel address in the Denver area and delivered me to the third. She had already checked me into the room so I was able to go directly there where a delightfully refreshing basket with my favorite snacks and beverage, together with other feminine amenities, awaited me. But this was only the beginning of my venture into the arena of Western hospitality!

Upon entering the fellowship hall, I was literally bedazzled by the beautifully appointed tables—each with its own theme chosen and executed by a hostess who used her creativity and resources to prepare the table and invite the guests. Apples became flag stands; place cards and napkin rings were personalized in cross-stitching on perforated paper; canned fruits and veggies or assorted bears or a wedding cake or even cowbells and porcelain cows were fashioned into interpretive theme tablescapes. Each table was unique. I was simultaneously drinking it all in, making notes, and hatching ideas of my own!

Since that initial experience, I have enjoyed similar invigorating creative forays across the country. Women have a unique gift for making the ordinary extraordinary and elevating the mundane to elegance. Such is creative hospitality—refreshing, inspiring, and contagious! And with the creation of websites such as Pinterest, the ideas are more accessible than ever. My favorite definition of hospitality is this: *You share what you are and what you have with no thought of what is in it for you.* Or, consider the admonition of the apostle Paul, "Share with the saints in their needs; pursue hospitality" (Rom. 12:13).

Interestingly, in the dictionary *hospitality* is wedged between *hospice* (a place of shelter) and *hospital* (a place of healing). Perhaps that is because ideally *hospitality* combines healing and shelter into one special ministry.

Comparing Christian Hospitality to Worldly Entertaining

Christian hospitality seeks to serve others, putting people before things, considering what is ours as yours, taking no thought of reward or compensation, and modeling itself according to the teachings of God's Word. It functions with a freedom that liberates. On the other hand, the world's entertaining wants to impress others, placing things before people, claiming what is ours is ours and wanting you to admire it, expecting reward and praise, squeezing itself into the world's mold as portrayed in magazines, on television, and in the opinions of others. It actually can become an enslaving taskmaster.

How to Be Hospitable

The essence of hospitality is a "heart open to God," and it begins at home (see Eph. 2:19–22). The Scriptures speak clearly about the methods of the hostess. She is to serve with love (Gal. 5:13); she is to offer her hospitality without grumbling (1 Pet. 4:8-10); she is to maintain calmness and self-control (Luke 10:41–42); she is to work energetically and heartily (Col. 3:23); she is to present her gift of hospitality "as something done for the Lord" (Col. 3:23). To invite someone into your home offers an opportunity to take the challenge of lifting that person's happiness quotient for as long as he or she is your guest.

The hostess becomes a steward of the resources of her home (1 Cor. 4:2). The major benefit of her wise stewardship and willing servanthood is the delight of serving. Time is the first resource, and it is given equally to all to appropriate as God directs. The psalmist calls on us to provide "food in due season" (Ps. 104:27 NKJV). Often you are tempted to take for granted the simple task of providing balanced, nutritious meals for your family and guests. When I am preparing a festive meal for family or friends, I try to set aside a block of time just to set my tables, design tablescapes, prepare place cards and favors, arrange china and flatware, fold napkins, and coordinate the entire culinary journey. On a really special occasion I may give as much time to these finer touches as to cooking the food.

Money is another resource (Acts 2:45), and you must work within your respective budgets. I have a hospitality closet in which I stockpile small gifts and supplies to be used in my hospitality ministry. Mini-Mexican sombreros, Oriental fans, shell leis, assorted baskets, biblical lampstands, and countless other "treasures" have been acquired, using strict economy and awaiting some creative use.

Energy must also be appropriated in any sincere efforts at hospitality (Titus 2:4). Whether preparing food, decorating tables, or planning activities, there is a price to be paid beyond dollars and cents. Over the years, as long as my health and other assignments permitted, I designed my own centerpieces from household accessories and equipment, usually made my own place cards and favors, and did much of my own food preparation. In this season of life, I am assisted by student helpers. Nevertheless, even with this help, putting a special function together is a tremendous investment of labor for me as well as my helpers.

Underlying the investment of time, money, and energy is the attitude of love. This love is action with feeling and feeling with action. No hostess will be ultimately effective unless she loves her guests.

Examples of Hospitality

Sarah was challenged to cook for angelic messengers (Gen. 18:1–8); so are we, but most of the angels who come to our tables are up in the air harping about something without a single garment of gratitude to wear! The Shunammite woman prepared a permanent guest room for the visiting preacher (2 Kings 4:8–10). When my daughter Carmen was young, she prepared delightful baskets of snacks and amenities for overnight guests in our home. Now she does the same in her home, assisted by her daughters—my gifted and service-oriented granddaughters Abigail and Rebekah.

Though married to a fool, the Old Testament hostess Abigail used gracious hospitality to usher her into the household of the king after her husband's death (1 Sam. 25:18–38). Paul enjoyed hospitality from many gracious women and took time to say thank you again and again (Acts 16:14–15). He also offered his own hospitality even in the most adverse circumstances; while under house arrest awaiting trial, he extended warm greetings and opened his Spartan quarters to all who came seeking his fellowship and presence (Acts 28:16–17).

Mary and Martha served drop-in lunch to a host of men (Luke 10:38–42); my joy is still to add students or campus visitors to our table on a moment's notice. During a visit to Easley, South Carolina, to enjoy fellowship with our dear friends and co-laborers Dorothy and Jim Merritt, we were invited to have an impromptu after-service supper in the home of Ronnie and Janet Metcalf, whom we had just met that very day. I felt that we were imposing to come for a meal on such short notice. However, I had but to walk into their gracious home to feel not only welcome but at home! Janet kicked off her "Sunday shoes" and went immediately to the kitchen. She had ordered three kinds of pizza to be delivered and had stopped at the grocery store en route home to pick up ingredients for a freshly made dessert—a delicious cherry cake topped with ice cream. As she prepared the dessert, she was simultaneously organizing a wonderful salad. She allowed us to help with chopping some of its ingredients, but she hovered over all, being sure that the meal was beautifully presented as well as carefully prepared. We all sat around the kitchen table and enjoyed a well-balanced and tasty supper and wonderful fellowship with new friends. And it all seemed so easy and natural for Janet!

Jesus is the very best example of hospitality. He frequently fed people; but even more important was His determination to go beyond the physical needs of His guests for food to offer answers to deeper needs of the heart and spirit in the midst of His genuine and complete hospitality (John 6:35).

The Guests in a Home

Jesus' guests, more often than not, were people with spiritual needs. You must remember your responsibility to invite people who do not know Christ into your homes. We have invited Moslems, Jews, and individuals who made no claim to be Christians to our table. The warmth of hospitality is a wonderful tool to open hearts to the gospel. Lonely people (the aged, bereaved, hurting) need to feel that someone cares. During our years in Dallas, an elderly widow with no family of her own joined our holiday festivities until her death. She continued to grow more feeble; she had difficulty hearing and seeing; she choked on her food and on occasion even regurgitated at the table in our home and in restaurants. Yet, even the young children in our extended family circle were kind and loving to her and reached out to make her feel loved and wanted because they did love her!

Those in the Lord's work should also be invited into your home, not only for your ministry to them but also for their ministry to you and your children. Over the decades we had a steady stream of preachers, missionaries, international Christian leaders, authors, and teachers; and our children, as we, were immensely blessed and edified by a touch with these committed and extraordinary men and women.

Friends will feel your love and experience your gratitude for them in a timely and effective manner as you offer your hospitality. Children must not be overlooked—the children of your friends, the children and youth of your neighborhood and your church, the children who are friends of your own children, and certainly not to be overlooked are the children you do not yet know whom God brings under your influence, even if only for a moment. I fed the high-school football team after every varsity game during my son's athletic career. I wanted to meet the needs of my own dear son; but I prayed too, that God would let me minister to the other boys, some of whom had no mother or father with any interest in their lives. God gave me a mission to make those boys feel loved and wanted through a rather simple ministry.

In the midst of all these guests, however, first and foremost in your heart should be your own inner family circle. Home must be the place to which you may return with eager spirits and sighs of contentment because you are loved and wanted there regardless of your reception elsewhere. To this day when I go to my mother's home—now in a lovely retirement center in New Orleans, Louisiana, I have a flood of memories from visits to our family home after I had left to establish my own home—a note of welcome on the kitchen blackboard and favorite foods in the refrigerator and on the bread block. Never have I made that trip home then or now when I did not feel loved and wanted!

The Rewards of Hospitality

"It is more blessed to give than to receive" (Acts 20:35). Sacrifices never go unnoticed (see Heb. 13:16). There are those times when you give of yourself unselfishly and untiringly without receiving a word of thanks. On such an occasion, one of the deacons in First Baptist Church, Dallas, handed me a card with this verse inscribed: "For God *is* not unjust to forget your work and labor of love which you have . . . ministered to the saints" (Heb. 6:10 NKJV). What an encouragement to know that God never overlooks what you do in His name, and how convicting to know that despite all you do in His name, God expects you to continue to minister (Matt. 25:14–30).

Frequently when I step from a public platform, a familiar face will approach me from the audience. A sweet young woman will remind me that she was in my home for one of our student functions (the salad supper for student wives, the high tea for wives of graduates, the Christmas receptions for students and faculty, the dinner for international students, etc.), and she will express her loving appreciation for the time and energies I expended to have some particular ministry. Or perhaps she will allude to the class I teach for students' wives and share something she learned and put to use in her own ministry. What a thrill to be used as God's conduit for ministry over the years and throughout the world!

Faithfulness in exercising hospitality can yield unusual and exciting benefits. Consider the men on the road to Emmaus who invited their companion (who turned out to be the Lord Jesus Himself) to eat with them. I remember with excitement accepting the assignment of managing a reception for a presidential candidate. It was a thankless task with countless headaches at the time, but I did my best. Some years later that candidate served as President of the United States, and as a result of faithfulness in other tasks, I had the privilege of serving as chairman of the Presidential Bible Committee during the administration of Ronald Reagan. With that assignment came a visit with the President in the Oval Office.

PART THREE

In Her Celebrations

22

Thanksgiving: A Focus on Gratitude

Giving thanks always for everything to God the Father in the name of our Lord Jesus Christ. (Eph. 5:20)

Thanksgiving is an American holiday appropriately initiated in the early days of our nation. No nation in history has enjoyed the affluence and prosperity that has characterized the United States of America.

How Do You Say Thanks?

The grateful acknowledgment of benefits received and blessings experienced constitutes an expression of thanks. You cannot experience this feeling of gratitude, however, without meeting certain conditions.

First, you must realize that the benefits have been bestowed or given, not earned or won. Many people in the world work harder and longer than you for a whole lot less. Ultimately, every good and perfect gift—blessing or benefit—comes from the Creator God (James 1:17).

Second, you must acknowledge that you are totally unworthy of the beneficence of the heavenly Father. You are not worthy of the death of Christ in your behalf (Rom. 3:10, 23; 5:8; 6:23). God's favor toward you is unmerited; you cannot earn and dare not demand His blessing.

Third, you must recognize that the blessings and benefits of the heavenly Father are great and manifold—actually beyond human understanding (Pss. 103:2–5; 107:8). Thankfulness is inextricably linked with unending joy and unceasing prayer (Phil. 4:4–6). Thanksgiving is an expression of joy for that which God has already given, and it anticipates a petition of prayer for what you still need. It is the center of your imperfect condition in which you receive blessings from God and make known your needs to Him. Furthermore, thanksgiving completes the divine circle: Blessings are given by God, and loving adoration is returned to the divine Giver by redeemed men and women.

What Do You Get from Saying Thanks?

Many by-products come from a grateful spirit. For example, gratitude produces freedom, courage, peace, satisfaction, and so forth. Worry, cowardice, strife, or unhappiness absolutely cannot coexist with a genuine spirit of thanksgiving.

A thankful spirit is also a sure comfort and defense in the midst of distress and tragedy (Jon. 2:1, 7, 9). There is always *some* cause for thanks, and *everything* offers a reason for thanksgiving (Rom. 8:28). The apostle Paul—the shackled man who with his co-laborer sang hymns of praise to God from a dark and desolate dungeon—certainly has a right to recommend to everyone the same attitude of grateful faith that he himself exhibited. After all, your thanksgiving does not spring from circumstances or people but from an immutable source—your own personal relationship to Jesus Christ (1 Cor. 6:11; Col. 3:17). Music sung without gratitude of spirit is hollow and heartless.

Some years ago I faced an unexpected serious surgery. Having already had several surgeries of the same type, I resented the fact that I had to go through the same ordeal again. My consternation was heightened by the fact that the late August timing meant that my children were preparing to enter school. My husband was in the midst of his busiest days with a faculty retreat and the student orientation for the fall semester. The surgery was a surprise. There was not even time to prepare and plan for the lengthy period of convalescence. However, the Lord used that very painful, agonizing experience to give me and my family many unexpected spiritual benefits.

> Therefore I take pleasure in infirmities, in reproaches, in needs, in persecutions, in distresses, for Christ's sake. For when I am weak, then I am strong. (2 Cor. 12:10 NKJV)

Personally, in my frustration and confusion, I was driven closer to God. I was compelled to search the Word more earnestly for comfort and peace in those difficult days; I was forced to receive the loving ministries of family and friends (a somewhat new experience for a preacher's wife who had busied herself with ministering to others). Countless blessings reached our family. For example, during those lengthy days of recovery our son, on his own initiative, began a personal quiet time. I, of course, had far more time for thoughtful introspection over the providence of God and His gracious hand, which is moving all the time in everything to care for you and me and to edify us. The Lord is the blessed controller of all things (1 Tim. 6:15). God's sovereign dispensation is a matter for gratitude and not for murmuring. It should provide a joyful forum and not a woeful dirge. It should prompt a happy attitude and not a bitter spirit.

> Trials must and will befall;
> But with humble faith to see
> Love inscribed upon them all,
> *That* is happiness to me.
> —Author unknown

Let me challenge you to enter every Thanksgiving season with your own expression of genuine gratitude of heart to the Creator-Redeemer—whatever your circumstances may be. After all, your trial of difficulty, or even your tragedy, may well be a benediction in disguise!

23

Love Worth Celebrating

Although an abstract quality and therefore indefinable as to precise meaning, "love" is often clearly visible, easily identified, and vividly portrayed in word and deed. Most dictionaries define the term as an emotion, a sentiment, or a feeling toward something or someone with the implication that the one who loves has little control over his feeling. However, Scripture describes love as caring, sharing, and serving, connoting action on the part of the one who loves.

A Caricature of Love

Typical of the world's love offerings are Elizabeth Barrett's *Sonnets from the Portuguese,* which were written to chronicle her own reactions to her friendship and love for Robert Browning. These sonnets have found their place in the world's literature as a tribute to that love. The Taj Mahal, a magnificent north

Indian alabaster mausoleum, was built as a death monument to Mumatz Mahal by her grief-stricken emperor-husband.

The head of John the Baptist on an ornate platter was the grisly gift requested by Salome and granted by Herod, who was infatuated with the young woman's sensual dancing. In the modern era, a million dollars of precious gems, along with a share of the Greek island Skorpios and $20 million spent in one year, were given by Aristotle Onassis for the pleasure of his bride Jackie Kennedy (both of whom are now deceased). Again, Scripture presents vastly different offerings of love—the widow who gave to the Lord the infinitesimal mites, representing all she had; the prince Jonathan, who offered to lay down his life for his friend David; and, finally, the greatest gift of love, which was made by our Savior Jesus Christ, who voluntarily laid down His life for you and me.

A Description of Love

Although Saint Valentine's Day is a pagan holiday, you can seize the opportunity to turn your heart and direct your energy to "love," which, according to Scripture, is the Christian's most important and desirable commodity, surpassing even faith and hope. Jesus condensed all Ten Commandments into two with "love" as the verb in both (Matt. 22:37–40). Love is prerequisite to being a good citizen, a caring neighbor, an attentive husband, a helping wife, or a nurturing parent (1 John 4:11).

Scripture declares that "God is love" (1 John 4:8). In other words, He is the Creator, the Example, and the Source of love. God's love is everlasting (Jer. 31:3), steadfast (Ps. 136:1), giving (John 3:16), and compassionate (Isa. 53:12).

The most extensive discussion of love is presented by the apostle Paul in 1 Corinthians 13:1–13. Paul begins by recapping the list of spiritual gifts—an oratorical tongue, a prophetic voice, an understanding heart, an enlightened mind, a mountain-moving faith, a gracious generosity, a sacrificial martyrdom (vv. 1–3)—all of which are worthless in comparison to the greater gift of love, a nonnegotiable essential in the Christian's character.

A homily describing in minute detail the apostle's understanding of love follows. Love is *longsuffering,* a word that might be used to describe someone who has been wronged yet who, though having the power to avenge the wrong, refuses to retaliate. The word does not suggest weakness but strength; it does not indicate defeat but victory. There is no better description of God's relationship to His children.

Love is kind, suggesting a sweet tenderness that anticipates the needs and desires of the beloved (Eph. 4:32). Love is content or satisfied (Prov. 5:19) and is willing to invest in another's happiness without expectation of return. The desire for the results of love is not as important as the willingness to share the sacrifice of love. Love is humility, the antithesis of pride, which is the essence of sin. The lover never ceases to be amazed and grateful that he is loved.

Love is wise, both courteous and charming in its reactions. Love is unselfish and without personal rights. Rollo May noted, "When we love, we give up the center of ourselves." The lover is continually thinking of her duties rather than rights; she is remembering responsibilities rather than privileges; she is never forgetting her gratitude for life rather than reminding others of what life owes her (Matt. 16:24–26).

Love is patient, willing to wait for God's timing and determined to obey God's laws (Song of Songs 2:7). Love is optimistic, always thinking the best and refusing to keep books on wrongdoing. Love is compassionate and full of mercy, covering imperfections and weaknesses with understanding and refusing to betray secret confidences.

Finally, love is certain, believing God and taking Him at His word that you cannot love Him unless you love His creation (1 John 4:20–21), and you cannot be obedient to Him unless you fashion your love after His. Love is courageous, bearing up under every trial, sustaining the assault of any insult, injury, or disappointment, and enduring every kind of persecution. Love is unfailing. Bound up in the immutable character of God Himself, it cannot end. God is the Creator-Designer of love; He is also the reservoir or source of love; He is the catalyst or orchestrator of love.

A Challenge to Love

You cannot begin or end love by personal whim or feeling. You achieve love by willfully developing in your own life the characteristics described above and by keeping your life hooked to the generator and source of power—God Himself. I do not cease loving a neighbor because that friend attacks or betrays me; a wife who loves her spouse with God's love cannot stop loving him just because their marriage has grown stale; a parent does not stop loving a wayward child.

Rather, genuine love is consuming, unconditional, and inexhaustible. It depends upon the lover and not upon the beloved, upon what you do volitionally and not upon how you feel emotionally, upon your inner attitudes and determination and not upon outward circumstances and pressures, upon the perfect *Yahweh* God and not upon imperfect men and women.

Why not make it your goal to express love in obedience to the divine mandate and as an impetus to life and growth for you. Reach out to family and loved ones with an unexpected call or visit, a loving embrace, some simple flowers, a favorite dessert, a few tender words. Look for new and exciting ways to say, "I love you."

24

The New Year: Resolutions with Purpose

Beginning a new year is an opportunity that you have experienced repeatedly and one that most of you will hopefully experience again. However, you will never have the opportunity to turn back to a particular year, a specific month, a certain week, or a given day. You cannot reclaim even minutes from an hour already begun so that "redeeming the time" does become very important. The opening words of Scripture are: "In the beginning God," and why not make that your theme as you begin anew each year.

Beginning the year with God is not like turning on your heating system at the onset of cold weather. Rather, a better comparison is the adjustment of the thermostat every day.

The psalmist wrote, "Evening, and morning, and at noon, will I pray, and cry aloud: and he shall hear my voice" (Ps. 55:17 KJV). This communion with God is not only a daily process but also the means of going through an entire day. Every believer, regardless of her spiritual sensitivity, depends upon some quiet moments alone with God on a regular daily basis.

When my husband and I went to seminary, we had the grueling schedule of a full load in theological studies, including Greek and Hebrew; we were serving an active pastorate in the city of New Orleans. I had taken three part-time jobs to ease our financial burden. In assessing my schedule for the day and noting that I spent four hours in the classroom studying the Bible and praying before each class and then another six to eight hours studying the Bible in preparation for those classes—not to mention regularly praying before every meal—I decided that the Lord would want me to add sleeping hours rather than having a personal quiet time. What a mistake! It never occurred to me to drop a class or say "no" to some request from my church or eliminate a part-time job. As a result, I completely broke my health and lost some precious years of spiritual growth.

The Lord has designed you for fellowship with Him. How do you have this fellowship? Many devotional tools are available to help you begin the new year with your own daily quiet time by adding to your regular format a plan for reading the Bible through in one year. If you have as much as a fifth-grade reading speed, you can read the entire Bible in eighty hours, which is a little less than half of the hours in an entire week! Some of you workaholics put in that many hours of hard labor in one week. However, a plan spread over a year's time suggests that you read three chapters each day and requires about fifteen minutes time or less than one percent of the day. That is not even a tithe of your time.

Brief devotionals designed to accompany the reading of Scripture may be used to supplement spiritual nurture. A focal verse may be chosen daily or weekly to memorize, or perhaps to mount on the refrigerator door or post in some other strategic spot. I have often done this in our home, and my daughter started Scripture memory and meditation with her daughters when they were young toddlers. The ultimate answer to every problem and the only perfect Word available in this troubled world comes from the Bible. Just reading God's Word will give you new purpose in living. Like King Josiah, you can begin "to seek . . . God" (2 Chron. 34:3).

In addition to a plan for reading through the Bible, you should also develop a prayer strategy that will enable you to undergird the ministry of your local church and mobilize your family prayer power for needs in your own home and beyond. Prayer calendars and journals are effective reminders of specific needs.

Personalize your own prayer calendar with family and missionary birthdays and personal needs. Make a note of answered prayers in which you have shared, as well as any testimonies from your family and friends concerning what God is doing.

With Joshua of old I say to each of you, "Today I will begin to exalt you in the sight of all Israel. . . . Come closer and listen to the words of the LORD your God" (Josh. 3:7, 9).

25

Christmas: A Holy Celebration

No time of the year calls forth any more excitement and joy than the Christmas season. As you begin to plan your family festivities, let me suggest some ways in which you can make the celebration of Christmas more meaningful to you, your family, and friends.

Announce

In the Greek New Testament, the word translated *gospel* literally means "good news." Most of you have far more contacts with people in December than any other month so your opportunities for witness are multiplied in that season. The holiday itself provides an apropos tool for witnessing, as you can share with clerks, merchants, friends, and loved ones the importance of Christmas as the birthday celebration of our Savior and Lord, Jesus Christ. The angel of the Lord had the privilege of giving the first birth announcement for the Christ child (Luke 2:9–14). You, too, can be "angels" or "messengers" of the Lord by announcing His coming to earth for your redemption.

Rejoice

The shepherds not only continued the spreading abroad of the good news of the gospel, but they also glorified and praised God (Luke 2:17–20). Christmas is an ideal time for rejoicing over the blessings bestowed upon all by the heavenly Father. Oh, that you and I might follow the admonition of the apostle Paul, "Rejoice in the Lord always" (Phil. 4:4). Make Christmas a holy celebration, feasting upon goodness and joy, despite the adversities and inconveniences that may occur.

Meditate

Mary, the mother of Jesus, pondered or meditated upon the events surrounding the birth of her first son (Luke 2:19). You, too, would do well to meditate upon the Lord's birth, His incarnation, His atonement, His life and ministry. In addition, remember those Christmas celebrations of years gone by—the traditions and festivities of your family during this joyous season.

Give

The "wise men" did not arrive to visit the Christ child immediately. Their journey was long and difficult. They came bearing gifts (Matt. 2:11). The Christmas season, above all else, should prompt you to lay a gift before the Savior. The tithe given through the local church is a divinely appointed minimum, and surely you would want to go beyond that to make a gift and offering to the Lord and His kingdom's work. Perhaps as my husband and I do, you make a gift to international missions, contribute to some ministry dear to your heart, or meet some special need of one less fortunate than you.

After you have given to the Lord, you will want to choose gifts for those whom you love, not in a perfunctory manner of exercising duty but as a loving expression of caring and sharing.

Make Room for Christ

The innkeeper had no room for the family of the Lord Jesus. How sad it is to see many people so caught up in buying gifts, writing cards, hanging decorations, baking goodies, and the like, that they have no time for the One whose birth is honored in the celebration of this wondrous season. God grant to each of you a determination to carry holy priorities into the busy holiday season and an emphasis upon keeping Christ in the center of Christmas.

26

The Christmas Season

Keep in mind the words of the Lord Jesus, for He said, "It is more blessed to give than to receive." (Acts 20:35)

This precious beatitude is so typical of the gracious Lord Jesus. Although not found in any of the four Gospels, its spirit is seen in Luke 6:38, "Give, and it will be given to you; a good measure—pressed down, shaken together, and running over—will be poured into your lap. For with the measure you use, it will be measured back to you." These words speak the heart and example of the Lord with marvelous clarity. Though the greater blessing lies in the right kind of giving, the implication is that it is also blessed to receive. The whole ministry of the Lord was giving, and the glory of the gospel is its unfolding of God's gift to man.

The Blind Side of This Admonition

How often have you given or tried to give in a spirit of love and compassion only to be rejected or ignored? Nothing cuts so deeply and leaves an ache so painful as spurned giving—whether it be an object carefully chosen or a deed lovingly planned.

Surely God has designed that the receiving of a gift or ministry should bless the one for whom it is intended—the receiver—just as much as it is a delight to the giver. Gratitude is the inspiration of heaven's most melodious anthems. Its fruit is joy in the time of mourning, courage in the day of despondency, security in the hour of loneliness, peace in the midst of the battle, and satisfaction in spiritual or physical famine. The writer of Ecclesiastes expressed it well:

> Two are better than one because they have a good
> reward for their efforts. For if either falls, his compan-
> ion can lift him up; but pity the one who falls without
> another to lift him up. Also, if two lie down together,
> they can keep warm; but how can one person alone
> keep warm? (Eccles. 4:9–11)

Apparently both profit from this mutual caring and love.

During the Christmas season, as perhaps no other, you can look forward with joyous expectation to receiving as well as to giving. Look at some important aspects of the opportunity for glorifying God, even through your receiving.

A Divine Ministry

In the first place, receiving assumes that someone has given. Scripture says, "Every generous act and every perfect gift is from above, coming down from the Father of lights; with Him there is no variation or shadow cast by turning" (James 1:17). God Himself inspires the giver. God knows more than you do about your needs. When you spurn a gift, you may well be rejecting a timely ministry inspired of God to minister to your own unique need.

One of my greatest delights is to extend hospitality to family, friends, and even to strangers. I always like to make plans, design invitations, prepare food, arrange tables, and I have never minded doing the cleaning up, using the time to relive in my own mind the joys of the time spent in investing in the lives of others. However, as days become busier, interests more diverse, and pressures more intense, I have discovered that sometimes I simply cannot do all I have planned. When friends offer to help, I sometimes resist, wanting very much to do it all myself—self-sufficient, independent, free from indebtedness to anyone. Yet, how sweet to relax and tear down my barriers, to receive assistance, to enjoy the security of camaraderie, to experience the success of partnership, to accept a gift of time, energy, or creativity even as one would accept a brightly wrapped package.

A Spiritual Exercise

Receiving is also profitable as a spiritual exercise. Receiving demands humility in recognizing your own need for help from another. You are admitting that you are not always adequate in yourself. It is the best way to learn gratitude.

God is the greatest Giver (John 3:16). If you spurn the gifts of your loved ones here on earth, how can you gratefully receive the gift of the heavenly Father? If you are a poor receiver here, you have failed the first step in learning gratitude for spiritual gifts.

A Loving Fellowship

The giver and receiver have a unique opportunity for fellowship with each other. There is an expression of love and a response of gratitude. There is an awakening of concern and a reply of delight. There is a giving of yourself and a receiving of another, which is the heart and essence of fellowship.

A Christmas Plea

Of course, you hear much about giving during the Christmas season, and I would not want to detract from that. Yet, let me also go on record as pleading for openness in the hearts of those receiving—whether husbands or wives, parents or children, friends or strangers. If someone wants to give you a selected gift or do a sweet deed for you, please do not look for excuses or apologies. Avoid the rejection of a gift lovingly given and refuse overlooking of a deed graciously done. Rather, extend your hand and open your heart; experience, enjoy, and accept creativity; express appreciation and feel gratitude. You, too, will be blessed, and you, too, will be ministering to another—perhaps even to one you love!

27

A Salute to Fathers for Faithful Servant Leadership

Anthropologist Margaret Mead once remarked, "Fathers are a biological necessity but a social accident." This flippant observation is certainly a far cry from the divine plan and mandate that assigned to the husband and father the responsibility of providing, protecting, and leading the family (see Gen. 2:15–17). God never planned for a father to become a poor substitute for the mother, performing her duties—though in an inferior manner—in her absence. Rather, fathers are equipped to make their own significant contribution to the care of infants or young children, whether sons or daughters, as well as teenagers, in their social, intellectual, emotional, and spiritual growth.

Studies of joint parental interaction with newborns have provided interesting insights. While mothers and fathers are equally involved even with newborns, they pursue their responsibilities differently. Fathers are usually more attentive and playful—talking to the baby and imitating the baby; but they are less active in the mundane tasks of changing diapers, feeding, and cleaning up the baby. In fact, the birth of a baby can revolutionize even the most egalitarian parents, pulling them back to traditional roles.

The Abdication of Some Fathers

In the past, fathers commonly were recognized as educators and guiding lights for their children. For example, consider the many popular television series such as *Father Knows Best, Make Room for Daddy, Bonanza,* and so forth. The father was portrayed as the leader and hero of the home. Unfortunately, many modern-day fathers teach their children what to do only by default. Millions of American children are being reared in fatherless families. Statistics have confirmed that delinquency abounds unchecked in fatherless homes.

Confusion over what is expected of a father is widespread. The mother has become the center around whom the family revolves, and the father has been enlisted as her personal assistant to help with chauffeuring, shopping, and any other task the mother delegates. Actually there is as much authority as ever in the heads of families, but now those heads are often women and/or children (see Isa. 3:4, 12). The defeat of a tyrannical father may be welcome, but beware the onslaught of the despotic mother.

Fathers have often stepped aside willingly, leaving their assignments without struggle or complaint. Abraham, when confronted with Sarah's bitter hatred for the slave-girl-concubine Hagar and her son, just acquiesced to Sarah's wishes, knowing that capitulation to her desires could well mean death to his own son.

Although the Scriptures strictly forbid this abandoning of responsibility by husband and father, there are countless godly men who honor the Lord in every area of life except in that sphere of leading wife and children through the family decision-making process. Nothing is any more devastating to a child than to see the authority of his father continually eroded away in the home. Some fathers abdicate their responsibilities and even abandon their families. Prayer is a powerful force for asking the Lord to turn a father's heart back home. Pray for extra wisdom for the mother who must fulfill roles of mother and father. Pray that the Lord might be a constant guide and comfort to children with absent fathers. Pray also that other godly men from the church and community will stand in the gap with loving guidance for these children.

A Challenge to All Fathers
A Christian Father's Ten Commandments

1. Thou shalt hold no other group more important than the family unit, in all thy ways being faithful to it.
2. Thou shalt teach thy sons and daughters to love, respect, and obey their parents.
3. Thou shalt be a loving and considerate husband.

4. Thou shalt not speak in a manner unbecoming to a Christian gentleman.
5. Thou shalt, by example, make Sunday a special day set aside for God and for worship as a family.
6. Thou shalt provide for thy family—spiritually and physically—in an adequate manner.
7. Thou shalt promote and lead family worship in thy home.
8. Thou shalt be honest in all thy dealings.
9. Thou shalt respect the desires and freedoms of thy family as individuals.
10. Thou shalt be the head of thy household, while ruling it with love.
   —Author Unknown

The God-honoring Christian father who chooses to take his responsibility seriously will devote tremendous effort and considerable time to being an effective parent. The father has opportunity to set before his children an example not only for tackling life confidently but also for relating to God. The child who learns a proper response to his father as an authority then finds it far easier to relate to the heavenly Father, to whom he has been introduced with anthropomorphic language in Scripture. The absence of an earthly father makes relating to your heavenly Father all the more difficult.

The Christian father gives his sons an example of godly manhood by assuming the responsibility for providing, protecting, and leading his family. When our son Armour was only four or five years of age, he noted his father's courtesies to me—opening doors, carrying bundles, and helping me with my chair. Without lecturing or prodding our son naturally proceeded to do the same. Our daughter Carmen has also been blessed because her relationship to her daddy was the training ground for the relationship she would have with her husband. Her father's tender affection and gentle kindnesses enhanced her feminine nature and prepared her to be a wonderful wife.

One of the greatest challenges for fathers is to find time for their children. Many men are prisoners of an obsessive work schedule. Some things cannot be bought by money or position. The time and interest needed by a child from his father, as well as his mother, on a regular basis is not found on any sale counter. Fathers are especially adept at providing fun times.

Epilogue to Children

Find ways to honor the unsung hero of your home and determine some means to express love and appreciation for the father of your children. Very probably he has borne the pressures of supporting your family even through difficult and lean years. Possibly he has denied luxuries to himself to provide for the family. Most assuredly, he needs your love and appreciation.

28

A Salute to Mothers for Unbounded Love

Many women have answered a most unique classified ad:

Woman wanted to help in house. 18-hour day. 7-day week. Sleep in. Must have experience in cooking, sewing, medicine, child care, and psychology, law, elementary electricity and household repairs, bookkeeping, marketing, and cleaning. Must be strong and willing with happy disposition. No wages. Room and board provided.

Motherhood is both a demanding and rewarding profession. There is no one on earth—no teacher, preacher, or psychologist—who has the same opportunity to mold minds, nurture bodies, and develop potential like a mother. The job, despite its pressures and difficulties, can be overwhelmingly satisfying and amazingly productive since the results of really competent mothering will be passed from generation to generation.

The Example of Those Who Have Gone Before

In the Old Testament, the godly Hannah prayed earnestly for a son. When her prayer was answered, she did not forget her vow to the Lord. Rather, she worked zealously to nurture her child and train him in the godly ways so he could serve the Lord all the days of his life. From childhood Samuel faithfully served the Lord with all diligence.

The Shunammite woman, who rejoiced in the gift of a son, cared for him lovingly. Upon his untimely death, because of her profound love for the child and her faith in the Lord, she traveled as quickly as she could to the prophet Elisha and persuaded him to come and restore her child to life (see 2 Kings 4).

Even Hagar, the slave girl, loved her son Ishmael devotedly. When they were sent into the wilderness, she cried unto the Lord for the sake of her child. God responded to the love of this rebellious, outcast mother (Gen. 16:8–13).

A mother can also wield over her child an enormous influence for the bad. The evil King Ahaziah of Judah, during his brief reign, was guided by his wicked and idolatrous mother Athaliah (2 Kings 8:26–27; 11:1–3).

In another era the beautiful and godly mother of John Chrysostom was widowed at a young age, refused many suitors, and committed herself totally to the responsibility of rearing her gifted son in the nurture of the Lord. He became the greatest orator of the early church. In a later generation,

Susannah Wesley, mother of John and Charles Wesley, turned aside from a public life of her own in order to rear and educate her children. She was incomparably brilliant and well educated; she herself could have attained professional success and perhaps even fame. However, she chose to pour her energies into rearing the large family God had given to her, and her sons shook two continents for Christ. On the other hand, one of the most cruel and bloodthirsty Roman emperors was Nero. He was marked for life by his murderous mother, Agrippina, in whose steps he followed.

History has verified that a mother can be the salvation or the destruction of her family. She plots its destiny in a unique sense. She can turn her household to good or evil, especially in the lives of her children, with whom she may spend countless hours.

Attributes of a Godly Mother

Every mother needs consistency in character and purpose. She cannot afford to zig and zag through life, making her decisions based upon the whim of a moment. She needs to be anchored in faith and commitment to the living Lord (1 Tim. 1:5).

A mother needs to be dependable and available with her first loyalty to husband and children and with a high priority for the home (Titus 2:4–5). Dorothy Canfield Fisher said, "A mother is not a person to lean on, but a person to make leaning unnecessary." Henry Ward Beecher remarked, "The mother's heart is the child's schoolroom." Every child needs the security of knowing that someone cares for him above every other earthly endeavor.

Another absolute for every mother is an unselfish and selfless nature. Mothers win most by losing all. By developing the Christlike quality of abandoning personal demands and rights and seeking to serve and minister to those whom God has provided for their own personal ministry, these unselfish heroines gain worth, wonder, and splendor beyond imagination. Abraham Lincoln often said, "All that I am or hope to be, I owe to my angel mother" (read Prov. 31:28).

Survival in motherhood also calls for a sense of humor. Close behind is the need for sensitivity to needs and for thoughtfulness issuing forth in comfort, kind deeds, and respect for personhood even when there is disgust for actions.

Challenge to Mothers

The coming generation will see no more pressing need than a revival of interest in the responsibilities of motherhood. Mothers need to be not only family-oriented but also family-obsessed. The family is not just *one* of a mother's responsibilities but should be *the highest priority* in her life. There is much talk about the virtue in childlessness and the fame in making your own place in the sun, but even in the midst of fading motherhood in the United States, you are hard put to locate a "graying mother" who believes that she made a mistake. You cannot pay a woman to do what mothers do for free. A mother has an irrational commitment, and she receives an intangible reward—not in materialistic benefits that fade but in blessings and honor that will last throughout eternity. In fact, I can honestly say, "Try it—you'll like it." That is the guarantee of the Lord Himself (cp. Ps. 127:3–5).

Epilogue to Children

Honor your mother, which is in keeping with the divine plan (cp. Exod. 20:12; Eph. 6:2–3). Shower her with tender affection and gentle courtesies, making her feel like the "very important person" she really is. Express to her in word and deed how much you love her. Notes of love will be deeply appreciated and long cherished. Thank the Lord for giving you a mother suited to your own special needs.

29

Romantic Love in Marriage: Mere Duty or Sweet Beauty

Everyone would affirm the prominence of love in Scripture, but perhaps some have not noted the presence of romance. Is there romantic love in the Bible?

Tradition has assigned to wives the undying desire for a lifetime of romance. As plants need sunshine and water, so a wife needs romantic love if she is to flourish and bloom. Marriage is not a destination but a journey, and romance paves the road of love in a beautifully lasting fashion.

The Ecstasy of Fellowship

The Creator God, who made the man and the woman, created in their souls this longing for fellowship and intimacy

(Gen. 2:18). If a man is denied this intimate fellowship, he usually buries himself in his work and finds a sense of fulfillment therein. On the other hand, the woman, whose life is designed to focus upon the home, is left with a void when her husband abdicates his responsibility for providing cherishing love.

The Lord Himself provided for romance of fellowship, not only in dating and courtship (cp. Song of Songs 2:8–17) but also in marriage (cp. Deut. 24:5). Most wives are very content to take their "year" of undivided attention in segments throughout a lifetime. The intimacy of fellowship does not come with the pronouncement that you are husband and wife or at the end of a certain number of years of marriage. Solomon, who had the experience of relating to one thousand women on a personal basis, wrote that you should not force the development of love or awaken love until love pleases (Song of Songs 2:7; 3:5). Can you make a flower bloom by pulling apart its petals? If you do try to force the bloom prematurely, you ruin the possibility of its ever becoming a beautiful and perfect blossom. Expressing love requires the investment of time. There must be lingering and unhurried expressions of thoughts and feelings released with unmeasured time for reflection.

The Element of Surprise

So Jacob worked seven years for Rachel, and they
seemed like only a few days to him because of his love
for her . . . and Laban gave him his daughter Rachel as
his wife. . . . Jacob slept with Rachel also, and indeed,

he loved Rachel more than Leah. And he worked for
Laban another seven years. (Gen. 29:20, 28b, 30)

Rachel was not surprised when Jacob asked for her hand
in marriage, but she must have been a bit startled by his willingness to labor seven years to win her hand. Then, through
Laban's trickery, Jacob was given Leah. Surely Rachel must
have given up hope of union with her beloved. The unexpected came, however, when Jacob labored yet another seven
years to receive his beloved Rachel.

An impromptu call to say "I love you," a frivolous gift
without occasion, an unexpected outing just for fun, a poem
or note of affection tucked away for your beloved to find—
these are examples of the unexpected. Truly you can express
love in a myriad of ways!

The Excitement of Creativity

Why let a marriage break up a beautiful romance begun
in courtship. For some, settling down in a rut within marriage before the honeymoon is over seems the easy path.
Unfortunately, the only difference between a rut and a grave
is the depth.

Women are often guilty of letting their companionship
and lovemaking become perfunctory. Note again the example
of Solomon, who describes the beauty of his beloved in poetry
(Song of Songs 4:17) and who takes her for walks in the for-
est (7:11–13), introducing creativity and romance into the
marriage.

The apostle Paul clearly states that the husband has
control of the wife's body (1 Cor. 7:4). The greatest control

a husband can have over his wife is through continuous, loving affection. Who knows what spontaneity would develop in marriage if husbands would give as much loving attention to their wives as they give to their cars, boats, businesses, hobbies, dogs, children, and the like?

The Enchantment of Frivolity

Love is like age; it cannot be hidden. You can give without loving, but you cannot love without giving. Your giving need not always have a price in dollars and cents. In fact, the best-received gifts are often those with the least monetary value, especially when it is the giving of yourself.

Beware of stifling romantic love by the determination always to be reasonable and practical. Being impractical on occasion is not always irresponsible. Perhaps a husband might invade his savings account to take his wife with him on a business trip that she would especially enjoy and during which they could have special time together.

Finally . . .

The Bible makes abundantly clear that God Himself designed the man and the woman with the capacity to enjoy romantic love—a love based upon fellowship, sharing, and intimacy. Human strength is not sufficient to empower this reservoir of energy found in romantic love (Song of Songs 8:6). In order to be able to understand each other and to love each other intimately as God designed, both husband and wife must have as the foundation for marriage a personal relationship with God upon which to build all other relationships.

If you are a woman married to an unbelieving husband, the challenge is greater and the stakes are higher. You must pray fervently for your husband's salvation. You also need to find a friend to walk with you in these difficult circumstances. The Lord can use your personal ministries to your husband as a tool of evangelism even when all else seems to fail (1 Pet. 3:1–4).

30

Traditions: Your Link to the Past and Anchor for the Future

At the heart of the Christmas celebration is the woman—wife, mother, grandmother. God has equipped her with special sensitivities for observing and studying the family and meeting the needs of each member, and God has assigned her the responsibility of keeping the home (Titus 2:3–5). This challenge becomes especially exciting and uniquely individualized during the Christmas season.

The psalmist wrote, "God provides homes for those who are deserted" (Ps. 68:6). The Hebrew word *yachid,* translated "deserted," may also be rendered "only one," "union," "isolated ones," "friendless," "wanderers," or "exiles." Every family does have its own unique God-given flavor and personality, and through the years each family builds a lifestyle and establishes traditions unique unto themselves, those marks that set them apart from other families and the common ground that draws them together as one unit. Christmas is a splendid season for the celebration of traditions, and who is more at the center of this happy time than a wife and mother?

Defining Tradition

Tradition is the handing down of information, customs, or beliefs from one generation to another or the inheriting of a certain pattern of thought or action. The former is passed down by willful determination through word of mouth or example, whereas the latter is more or less absorbed by the process of osmosis. God's instructions to parents concerning the rearing of their children include both methods. For example, there is the direct command to teach spiritual truths by word and example (see Deut. 6:4–9) within one's household and the indirect reminder from the heritage of faith, which reinforces teaching and example (see 2 Tim. 1:4–5) throughout the generations. Traditions blend with daily routines and individuals to produce a lifestyle and ancestry to be passed on generation after generation (Pss. 71:18; 78:4–7).

Remembering Traditions

Christmas traditions are special to the Patterson household, and I remember the godly women in my own life who have helped to make Christmas meaningful. My paternal grandmother Grace Kelley made all her Christmas gifts. They were practical, yet very unique, and represented an investment of her time and energies. My sister Kathy through the years has lovingly prepared bright-red, felt Christmas stockings, whose beaded and sequined decorations were personalized for the particular members of the family. With the next generation, Aunt Kathy's labor of love has continued to delight our Christmas Eve ritual of hanging the stockings.

My mother has always been at the very heart of our Christmas festivities! She bakes cookies, cakes, and candies for weeks and weeks. Her baking goes beyond the family circle to friends, teachers, and employees. Her children learned early that Christmas was a time to express love and gratitude. Mother has consistently delighted and reveled in Christmas decorations and has spent countless hours making the house beautifully festive both within and without. She always encouraged the compiling of Christmas lists and searched for extraordinary gifts and treats over a period of time. Perhaps her greatest Christmas treat, however, was the scrumptious Christmas brunch served on Christmas morning. Her preparations began the evening before and continued in the early morning hours so the entire "Kelley Clan" could enjoy eggs and sausage, homemade biscuits and gravy, grits, and even more.

Then I remember my husband's mother, affectionately known as "Honey." She always showed unequaled flexibility and adaptability to the uncertain and erratic schedules of her ministry family. The Christmas celebration was planned for whenever we could all be present, whether before or after or on Christmas Day itself. She always surprised us with a spectacular and exotic Christmas dinner of unusual delicacies skillfully prepared and set upon a lovely, well-appointed table.

For many years she lovingly designed the family Christmas card, which sent a greeting of love to friends around the world. I especially remember the year that Honey enhanced all her Christmas cards with flowers lovingly fashioned from tiny shells she had gathered along the Texas coast. They were prepared with special card stock to become ink blotters!

Establishing Traditions

From this blessed heritage, I have the privilege of pulling together Christmas traditions for this generation's family circle, traditions through which my husband and I have enriched our children and grandchildren. Several goals stand out in my planning:

- I, as wife and mother, am determined to be involved in the planning of Christmas festivities in my home. I want to invest my time and energies making the season special to my family.

- I want to give my children and grandchildren, as well as nieces and nephews, memories of my doing special things for them; baking goodies beautiful to see, aromatic to smell, and delicious to taste; decorating the house with a tree and ornamentation; making private purchases and giving an air of joyous mystery.

- I want to pass on to my children a spirit of giving gifts to express love and gratitude to those whom they love and admire—family members, teachers, friends, and classmates.

- I want to remind my children of the love and joy bound up in home and family—not only the excitement of exchanging gifts but also the fun of singing carols and laughing together, the comfort of companionship and love.

- I want to instill in my family an understanding of the true meaning of Christmas, a realization of the genuine Christmas spirit that focuses on the giving of yourself as well as the receiving from others, undergirding all with love for the Savior whose birth we celebrate.

Conclusion

Christmas is a wondrous time for families; a sentimental season to draw in the extended family from their scattering throughout the land; a period to think of others and to give expression to love; a time to eat at home as a family, enjoying culinary masterpieces reserved for special occasions. Christmas is an exciting, festive occasion with colorful decorations, delectable food, and melodious music; it is an altruistic opportunity for an outpouring of your energies and the channel for bestowing gifts and remembrances; it is a spiritual celebration to point hearts and minds to the Creator-Father God whose heavenly gift of the Savior-Son, the Redeemer, surpasses all human philanthropy and earthly generosity.

PART FOUR

In Her Service to God and Country

31

Christian Courtesy—
Doing the Acts of Love

Be kindly affectionate to one another with brotherly
love, in honor giving preference to one another. (Rom.
12:10 NKJV)

An Axiom for Christian Courtesy

Throughout the New Testament clearly the Christian life
is not merely doing certain things but rather a certain manner
of doing everything, according to my friend Mary Crowley.
This exhortation from the pen of Paul is a direct word to every
believer. The reference to "brotherly love" obviously goes
beyond the strong natural affection between parent and child
and among siblings within the family. This tender love can be
emulated in the interpersonal relationships of Christians one

for the other with the same sincerity and tenderness as if they were bound together as the nearest of relatives. The Greek word translated *preferring* means "to go before" or "to lead" and thus is a reference to the example you are to set. Instead of waiting for others to honor you, you are to lead out and initiate every courtesy.

The Attitude of Esteeming Others

. . . but in humility consider others as more important than yourselves. (Phil. 2:3)

Polite behavior goes far beyond the observance of certain traditional modes of behavior or the practice of prescribed rules in your daily lifestyle. Volumes have been written on this subject for every generation, as both customs and culture have undergone various changes in what we say and do in daily living. The New Testament again cuts to the core of the matter in emphasizing the attitude of the heart toward your family, friend, or acquaintance. Without a considerate regard for others, there is no motivation for practicing common courtesies nor is there inspiration for instructing yourself in the common acts of thoughtfulness that are destined to afford comfort and happiness for others.

On an occasion when Queen Victoria was entertaining royalty at her castle, fifty guests of nobility, all in their finest garments, were seated around the banquet table. One of the guests from another country and culture did not understand the function of the finger bowl, which was near his place setting. Finally, he proceeded to lift it to his lips and drink from it. The queen, who was also a wise and observant hostess, watched him drink the bitter lemon juice mixture. Rather than have her guest suffer discomfort or embarrassment, she promptly picked up her own finger bowl and drank its content. The other guests followed suit, not daring to question the judgment or action of the queen. The queen had broken the rules of etiquette, but in so doing she avoided lowering the esteem of her guest and set a standard for kindness that has long been remembered.

The Action of Gracious Hospitality

Let brotherly love continue. Don't neglect to show hospitality, for by doing this some have welcomed angels as guests without knowing it. (Heb. 13:1–2)

The writer of Hebrews wisely begins with a reminder that brotherly love is at the foundation of all hospitality. There is probably not an art any more lost to this generation than that of homespun hospitality—meeting the needs for food and lodging of those whom the Lord may send to your home.

Challenge

Make your commitment to extend hospitality to family and friends, to keep the welcome mat out and the coffee pot ready. Then move within the home in a renewed effort to practice common courtesies to one another at the table, without interruption from the telephone and other electronic devices, in conversation, in thoughtful gestures, and in multiplied kindness. My son Armour in his youth began his quest to become a gentleman in full bloom. Since early childhood, he has showered upon his mother the common courtesies that accentuate my femininity and showcase his manliness. He did not learn these in the classroom or from a book but from the example of a gracious father who practiced the humble acts before his observant son.

32

Responsibilities in Citizenship: Standing in the Gap

[9]Rise up, you women who are at ease,
Hear my voice;
You complacent daughters,
Give ear to my speech.
[10]In a year and *some* days
You will be troubled, you complacent women;
For the vintage will fail,
The gathering will not come.
[11]Tremble, you *women* who are at ease;
Be troubled, you complacent ones;
Strip yourselves, make yourselves bare,
And gird *sackcloth* on *your* waists. (Isa. 32:9–11 NKJV)

This world is on the brink of destruction in every area of life. In government there is deceit, bribery, and scandal on every hand. In the moral arena, millions of babies have been murdered by abortion. In fact, in some major cities there were more deaths by abortion than there were live births!

A rapidly developing welfare state makes it more profitable to do nothing than to work—another direct violation of Scripture (see 2 Thess. 3:10). The nation's economy is on the verge of bankruptcy as money becomes valueless and as savings decrease in appreciation because of inflation. Government seemingly is being manipulated by radicals and their demands, and godly counsel is seemingly absent among those who govern the land. In the religious world is raging a cancerous and deadly attack under the guise of righteousness as some religious leaders cry "peace when there is no peace."

The United States is distinctive among the nations of the world in that it was founded upon the principle of "In God we trust." From its inception, this republic has been proud of the righteous principles contained in its Constitution and honored by its founders and leaders.

The New Testament does not neglect civic responsibility, which is clearly delineated in Romans 13:1–6. The task of Christian citizenship is based upon this teaching from the New Testament:

- Government is ordained and established by God Himself (v. 1). Therefore, to seek to remove Him from it is ludicrous.
- The purpose of government, through the work of its elected officials, is to curtail evil in the world (v. 3).

- The task of government includes the punishment of evil men, including capital punishment (v. 4).
- Christian responsibility includes supporting the government through tribute or taxation (v. 6).
- Subjection to the government is required of all believers for the sake of conscience as well as to avoid wrath (v. 5). However, because the people of the United States of America *are* the government and because its citizens pay the bills of the government's work, they are under divine mandate to make their government fulfill its divinely given assignment. As His trusted steward, your responsibility to God is to elect wise, honest, God-fearing men and women to public offices and to support them in the enacting of just and noble laws.

This call to the women of America is echoed from across the countless generations through the pen of the eloquent prophet Isaiah. Just as the women of Jerusalem, the women of this generation must accept the responsibility for having been "careless," a word connoting far more than a carefree spirit. Rather, the reference is to women with a false confidence as to their security, women who naively believe themselves to be protected from harm, women who unwisely refuse to recognize coming danger, women who are at ease in luxury and plenty (see Amos 6:1).

When the women of a country are lulled into apathy and lack of concern for the welfare of their nation, the condition is tragic indeed. However, you *can* hear the prophet of old, through whom the Lord speaks to you today. You *can* arise and do the very opposite of what you have been doing. You *can* rebuke your lethargy and indifference and change your attitude. You *can* awaken and act!

There are an estimated forty million evangelical Christians in the United States. Recent surveys indicate that 50 to 70 percent of evangelicals do not vote, and 30 percent are not even registered. These evangelicals, if they are worthy of the name, are committed spiritually and morally to doing what is right and righteous. Therefore, they must arise, take note of the issues, seek information on candidates and platforms, commit themselves to the battle, and enlist others to join with them. Nothing will turn the battle at a critical moment like the arrival of fresh, well-trained troops. Women, we *can* do it!

Are you looking for proof to encourage you? Note the humiliating defeat of the Equal Rights Amendment, despite the expenditure of huge amounts of government money, the tremendous influence from many high and mighty government and religious leaders, and the illegal and desperate changing of rules in midstream. Yet God raised up Phyllis Schlafly and Beverly LaHaye and countless thousands of other godly women determined to become active and responsible citizens. Note the reversal of the Supreme Court on the abortion-on-demand issue. Again, money, power, and influence were overwhelmingly against the anti-abortion, pro-life cause. Yet a group of women like Dr. Mildred Jefferson, Dr. Carolyn Gerster, and countless thousands of the rest of us arose. I am so proud of my denomination, the Southern Baptist Convention, for passing a strong and clear resolution, putting us on record as being pro-life and anti-abortion.

Instead of increasing government control in every sector, including education and religion, every Christian must recognize and return to the divinely assigned responsibilities of citizenship. Return to the family the responsibility for nurturing and educating children (Deut. 6:4–9). You do not want the state to control the church or the church the state. However, this principle of separation of church and state, which was designed as a means of protecting religious liberty, has been remolded by secular humanists to attack and undercut individual liberty, taking God out of government and beating down God-fearing people, thereby turning the nation toward becoming an atheistic and amoral nation.

Instead of government welfare, God admonishes Christians to share with those physically unable to perform meaningful work (1 Cor. 16:1–3). Instead of abortion, which is strictly forbidden in Scripture (Exod. 21:22), the Creator God established a high and reverent view of human life. This sanctity of human life demands the establishment of responsibility for a man and a woman who dare to enter the sacred and intimate union designed and engineered by God Himself without recognizing God's boundaries and accepting divine responsibilities. Without abortion on demand, there would be no need to usurp God's creative power through the test tube, nor would you find yourself swallowed up by the godless powers of the world because of the continuing decline of the birth rate in the United States, nor would the nation have countless families without children and without even the option of adoption because there are not enough babies available.

Without a doubt, Christian women who are interested and informed *can* make the difference in the future of

America. From biblical times until the present hour, women have been changing nations for the good or the bad.

Here is the game plan:

- *Pray* as you have never prayed before for your country and for the people who have the power to change its direction.
- *Inform* yourself by reading, listening, and observing, and seek counsel from godly people who are informed about the state of the nation.
- *Enlist* other women to stand with you in a renewed commitment to meaningful citizenship.
- *Vote* in elections on every level. Let nothing stand in your way. Encourage friends and neighbors to do the same.

Citizenship and its duties are God-given responsibilities that are not optional or transferrable. Women, you can make a difference in calling our nation back to God!

33

Evangelism: Every Woman's Kingdom Job

The caption of a familiar cigarette commercial once read, "You've come a long way, baby." The question in many minds is, "A long way to what"?

Women today are commonly seen smoking and drinking; they are often heard cursing. They frequently leave their husbands, complaining: "He doesn't pay the bills"; "he is too sick to handle his responsibilities"; "he's never been a good father"; "he doesn't meet my sexual needs"; "he's a hindrance to my career"; or "I don't love him anymore."

Many women have demanded abortion as a tool for birth control and through legislation and manipulation have sought to assure themselves of personal rights. There is also a mass exodus from the home by wives and mothers, accompanied by rising rates of juvenile delinquency, pregnancy out of wedlock, and so forth. There is no more strategic task before this generation than winning women to faith in Jesus Christ and establishing a sure foundation to which they can cling in times like these.

The Problems That Beset Us

Since Eve fell prey to the tempter in the garden of Eden, women have been oppressed by problems and difficulties. Boredom rates high on the list. Many women do not find in their homemaking tasks the mental stimulation and creative outlets they desire. They feel trapped, martyred, and bored. They leave the home seeking "greener pastures" only to find another problem—fatigue, one of the most devastating enemies a woman ever faces. Women who work excessively without proper rest will pay the price in body, mind, and temperament. Another problem often uniquely associated with women is worry, since most are determined to seek their own ways of dealing with their woes and troubles. Now, the bottom line on all these problems is a woman's rejection of the absolute principles God has provided for her in His Word and the determination to refuse to be obedient to God-given authorities in her life. This conclusion carries you to the starting place for ministries to women. Women need Jesus Christ as Savior and Lord of their lives, and God has directed born-again women to share the good news.

Prerequisites for Evangelism

The first prerequisite for an evangelist is a genuine salvation experience in which you have come to know Jesus Christ personally (1 John 1:1–10). This is followed closely by a love for Christ and for the people of the world—even those who are unlovable (2 Cor. 5:14). Then you must be willing to be used by the Holy Spirit since He is the One who convicts the soul and works regeneration (John 16:8). These first three prerequisites are simple compared to those remaining.

The first major roadblock appears with the call to live a separated life (2 Cor. 6:17; Rom. 12:12), for holiness of life or set-apart living is where the water hits the wheel. This not only suggests an added activity but also demands a changed life governed by biblical principles and controlled by the individual's willing obedience to God's written Word. Though you can claim direction by the Holy Spirit for almost any lifestyle, you can show and demonstrate divine guidance only by straightforward and unwavering obedience to the living Lord.

Another not-so-easy task is the creativity to use every opportunity for speaking a word for Christ (1 Pet. 3:15). For example, the one sitting next to you on the airplane is a captive audience for the gospel. The one who does your hair is a mission field you visit periodically. During holiday seasons, such as Easter, everyone with whom you meet or do business is an opportunity to share the good news of the resurrection.

Finally, the responsibility for sharing your faith costs you time beyond the actual minutes required to present the plan of salvation and your testimony. Never underestimate the necessity for preparation of heart and direction of spirit that come in the quiet moments of personal devotional time. The study of God's Word must precede understanding the Scriptures and realizing the ability to explain the way of salvation (Ps. 51:13; 1 Pet. 2:2), and definite and unceasing prayer must bathe the life of one who wants to be a soul-winner (1 Thess. 5:17).

The Challenge to You

Women have been involved in sharing the good news of the gospel since the days of the early church. Mary Magdalene was first at the tomb and the first to proclaim the victory of the Lord's resurrection. The first evangelist to the Jews was also a woman—the prophetess Anna, who, upon seeing the Christ child, immediately began to proclaim redemption to Israel.

Will you join me in a renewed commitment to share the living Christ at every opportunity? In the home, women have the opportunity for a life testimony to husband, children, and even neighbors and friends whom God may send to their respective havens of rest and shelter. In the church, they have the challenge from the apostle Paul to reach the younger women (Titus 2:3–5); they have the example of Lois and Eunice in teaching children (2 Tim. 1:5); and they have Priscilla's precedent for personal teaching and disciplining of young and immature Christian workers (Acts 18:26).

Women also have unlimited power and resources available in preparation through prayer and Bible study (Ps. 119:9–11). Then, there is the avenue of proclamation. Philip's daughters prophesied or proclaimed publicly the good news under the direction of their godly father, and Naaman's young maid shared her testimony privately with those in her household.

In the community, women have the ministry of hospitality, which Mary and Martha used so effectively, and the witness in the business community, which Lydia determined to utilize. Finally, the Samaritan woman at the well shared her own personal testimony with her friends and townspeople, something every woman can do. If you are redeemed, then you have a testimony of what Christ has done in your own life and what He continues to do daily.

34

Ministries in the Church—Woman to Woman

The inspired writers of Holy Scripture used family terms and concepts in teaching how to relate to God. Yahweh is described as the heavenly Father, and believers are called sons and children of God, joint heirs with Jesus Christ. The church is delineated as the bride, and Jesus is the Bridegroom. Alongside the scarlet thread of redemption is a hallowed thread of home life, which begins in Eden with the first family and continues on through the Bible. The home is God's picturesque illustration to mankind of His perfect love as portrayed in the Father, the dramatic stage for complete sacrifice as shown in the Son, and the object lesson for His illuminating teaching through the Holy Spirit.

Without godly homes, there would be no churches. When Paul wrote to Titus concerning the church in Crete, together with the instructions on the qualifications and duties of pastors and the exhortation to godly living, he included a directive to women (Titus 2:3–5). That directive has as its foundation the development of character to provide a godly example of life and to direct the concentration of energies and talents toward establishing a godly home and haven through which the love of Christ and His message of redemption can be passed on to family members.

A threefold purpose adds urgency to this teaching:

- to guard the sanctity of the home (Titus 2:4–5);
- to prevent blasphemy of the Word of God (Titus 2:5); and
- to give young women opportunity for exciting spiritual ministry (Titus 2:12–15).

The first block in developing the role of women in the church is the understanding that a woman's work in the church begins with submission and honor in the home.

The woman was created to be a helper perfectly suited for the man. This indicates an intimacy of fellowship (Gen. 2:24), the strength of two with supplementation and complementation in spiritual responsibilities (Eccles. 4:9–12) and a unity of purpose of one-mindedness (2 Cor. 13:11). The teaching and pattern of the New Testament concerning the woman's role in the church does not violate God's divine order in the home; rather it displays complete harmony. The basic role relationship of the male and female in marriage was established long before there were teaching and ruling functions in the church.

In that relationship there is both equality and difference, according to God's Word (Gen. 2:18).

If equality of essence or personhood and position in Christ means uniformity and the erasure of differences in office and role, subordination within the Godhead would also be negated. However, the Son is clearly obedient to the Father and thereby glorifies Him (Phil. 2:5–8; John 6:38; 8:29; 14:13, 28). The Holy Spirit is assigned the task of testifying of the Son and glorifying Him (John 15:26; 16:13–14). Yet, there is specific emphasis on the equality in the Godhead (John 10:30). All scriptural teaching concerning the triune God and the principles and practices of church government and leadership are in harmony. Men and women are equal in value; both are created in the image of God (Gen. 1:27). Yet each is distinct in role and responsibility (Gen. 2:15–18), as is modeled in the Godhead. Jesus, who is equal to the Father, is submissive to Him (John 15:28; Phil 2:6–8). God the Father loves the Son (John 15:9) and sends Him forth (John 16:5), and the Son responds accordingly (John 4:34; 6:38; 14:9) in His role as the agent of redemption. The Holy Spirit is God in you, indwelling the believer to do the divine work within the human heart (John 16:5–13), and He glorifies the Son (John 16:14).

Therefore, equality of spiritual privilege does not nullify the principle of subordination, established in the home at its inception in Eden, reiterated as applicable in both home and church structure in the New Testament, and exemplified in the relationship within the trinity of the Godhead. Paul mentioned many women with favor and did not hesitate to employ women in the service of the gospel (Rom. 16:1–4;

Phil. 4:3; Acts 16:14, 40). Clearly, God expects the married woman to give her first energies to a husband and home, whereas an unmarried woman with the gift of celibacy can give her entire life and energies to the work of the Lord outside the home (see 1 Cor. 7).

First Timothy 2:9–11 is not a general, blanket prohibition eliminating the woman from teaching and leadership but rather a qualified prohibition clarifying and paralleling organization within the church so that it is in harmony with the divinely appointed relationships in the home. Accordingly, a woman is not to teach or to exercise authority over a man in the church. This prohibition cannot be ignored as being merely cultural because divine order in the home was not established to conform to the cultural tradition of a particular people or to a specific era of history but rather to God's timeless principle for Christian marriage (Gen. 2:24). The application of this principle is not restricted to women who are married—a wife and her husband—since the larger context gives no confirmation of such narrow limitation but rather gives some evidence of God's design for the man and the woman based upon their respective natures.

First Corinthians 14:33–35 is set in the midst of a chapter in which the apostle speaks authoritatively concerning the use of spiritual gifts. To test the value of each gift, he uses the norm of whether or not the gift edifies or builds up (vv. 4–5). Again, Paul finds in the Corinthian congregation circumstances that prompt him to emphasize the divine order to be honored, not only by speakers and prophets but also by women.

Conclusion

In summary, then, in the Bible and in the early Christian community, teaching concerning the role of women in the church is plainly based upon God's divine order for the home—submission to and honor of the husband by the wife. Through obedience to this divine command the woman attains her ultimate reward. In her sphere of the home, the woman is to be honored and her talents used within and without, yet never allowing herself to be detracted from her primary responsibility to husband and children and the keeping of the home.

In addition to her teaching ministry in the church, which is to be done according to biblical guidelines, the woman is given the opportunity for a ministry of hospitality to the saints as an outreach of Christian love (John 12:1–11). Women have a unique opportunity for individual ministries because of the sensitivity and intuition with which God endowed them (Acts 9:36–43; 18:2–3, 26).

May the day never come when the church is without either the man or the woman. I fervently pray that women will always work within the clear authority of His Word, neither seeking recognition nor demanding higher office but making every effort to serve the Lord Jesus and trusting the providence of God to open opportunities and give them usefulness beyond their limitations and expectations.

35

Will the Real Evangelical Woman Please Stand Up?

The term *evangelical* has been used to label many diverse entities: denominations, theological postures, individuals, schools, churches, methodology, etc. Its etymology evolves from the Greek term *euaggelion* (prefix *eu,* meaning "good," and noun *aggelia,* meaning "message" or "news"), with its most simplistic definition being related to the gospel as found in the New Testament. To quote my favorite theologian, Paige Patterson, "An evangelical is an individual holding the traditional orthodox views relating to the major doctrines and looking to the Bible as the sole authority for faith and practice."

Since the present-day theological battleground is in the realm of semantics, a mere definition, however clearly stated, is not sufficient to separate the genuine evangelical from a "pseudo-evangelical," who talks the right lingo and infiltrates the right groups, while knowing in his heart that he does not belong to, nor is agreeable to, nor is in the spirit of the gospel or teachings of the New Testament.

Whether consulting a secular unabridged directory or searching through a dictionary of theological terms, you will note these distinctives associated with the designation "evangelical":

- the authority of Scripture,
- a personal conversion experience through the atoning death of Jesus,
- the importance of preaching as contrasted with ritual, and
- a character marked by missionary evangelism.

Theological resources are more precise in setting forth those doctrines marking the evangelical posture: namely, the plenary inspiration of Scripture, the deity of Christ, the acceptance of miracles as recorded in Scripture, the vicarious suffering and death of Christ as a complete and efficacious atonement for sin, the reality of His victorious resurrection from the grave and ascension to heaven, and the assurance of His imminent coming again.

The question here is: Are you an evangelical woman? If so, what entitles you to that designation?

The Authority of Scripture

The most important issue debated among those who call themselves evangelicals is the crux of biblical authority. A genuine evangelical woman is committed to the authority of Scripture as the written word of God, without error and infallible in its original autographs, completely reliable to every generation as a guide for faith and practice. All other doctrines stand or fall according to your position on this tenet.

In the garden of Eden, Eve began her fall into sin when the tempter persuaded her to question the Word of God, "Did God really say . . . ?" (Gen. 3:1). Every area of testing has such a trapdoor, through which many a good woman has fallen when the principles expressed in Scripture seem unpalatable to her personally or out of step with modern times.

Sarah had been given God's word about the promised heir and son to be born to her and Abraham in their old age. Even so, Sarah questioned God's promise, and this began her fall into the clutches of the tempter with the resulting heartaches that ensued. She gave her handmaid Hagar to her husband to produce a son and then with jealousy and bitterness despised both mother and child and lost confidence in her husband for his abandonment of the leadership responsibility given him by God and for his spineless acquiescence to her unwise whim.

There is not a more crucial characteristic of the evangelical woman than that she be committed to priorities as determined by divine assignment:

- a personal relationship and intimate fellowship with God through the daily quiet time with its private prayer and Bible study (Matt. 6:33);
- her responsibility as wife and helper to complement her husband (Gen. 2:18);

- her opportunity as mother and nurturer to rear her children in the Lord (Titus 2:4); and
- the investment of her own unique talents and abilities in ministries beyond the family and home (Prov. 31:20, 26).

The woman's role is defined by the clear principles found in Scripture. For example, note the equality of essence in the personhood of every believer regardless of race, sex, or status (Gen. 1:28; Rom. 8:17; Gal. 3:28; 1 Pet. 3:7), paralleled by the difference in official function as seen in the creative act itself (Gen. 2:18–25), as simply reiterated in biblical principle (1 Cor. 11:1–12; Eph. 5:21–33; Col. 3:17–18; 1 Pet. 3:1–7), and as exemplified in the Godhead. The Father, Son, and Holy Spirit are one, and each is equally God (John 1:1; 5:23; 14:6–7, 9, 11; 10:30, 38).

On the other hand, official responsibility showing difference and distinction, not inferiority, in the respective function and office of each is also clearly assigned (John 4:34; 5:19, 30; 6:38; 8:28–29, 54; 10:17–18; 14:28, 31; 15:26; 16:14; 17:2, 4–5; Phil. 2:5–11). All believers stand equally before God; but as responsible members of the body of Christ, they are governed by those in authority over them, whether it be a husband in the home (Eph. 5:22; Col. 3:17; 1 Pet. 3:1) or a civil authority in government (Rom. 13:1–5) or a pastor in the church (Heb. 13:7, 17). In addition to the authorities God has placed over you, He has also given you plain principles in His Word to define those authorities.

How appalling to see someone twist and distort Scripture, implying that humanity, or those created by the Creator,

have advanced beyond and even surpassed the all-wise God
and His Son who is Wisdom personified, maintaining that in
this world marked by heartache and immorality, violence and
anarchy, injustice and apathy, you could find a better paradise than Eden itself. How can you suggest that you malign
the integrity and character of God Himself, stripping the
love of God of its righteousness and justice to allow distortion, undercutting, and complete disregard for the authority
of Scripture? Some even pay for the propagation of these
heretical teachings with the tithes and offerings of God's
people (Gal. 1:6–9). How tragic to encourage self-centered
and self-serving reversals of the assignments God made in
the home because His creation has allegedly come up with
"something better" than God's best! How shocking it is to
permit the blatant and unrestrained parade of homosexual-
ity not only in the community but also in the church and
its officers under the guise of Christian love (Lev. 20:13;
Rom 1:24–26; Jude 7) and to allow the sanctity of life to be
violated because of inconvenience, irresponsibility, or selfish-
ness (Exod. 21:22–24; Ps. 139:13; Jer. 1:5).

The Beauty of Life

An evangelical woman who has experienced regeneration and who is committed to the authority of Scripture, will
bloom with the beauty and fragrance of the Christian life.
This woman is controlled by the Holy Spirit, who not only
has become a permanent resident in her heart at conversion
but who also controls her life by His filling again and again
(Eph. 5:18). Being controlled by the Spirit and walking with
Him, the genuine evangelical woman reveals the unique fruit

of the Spirit—"love, joy, peace, patience, kindness, goodness, faith, gentleness, self-control" (Gal. 5:22–23). Her life is further marked by prayer and Bible study, which give spiritual sustenance and growth.

Evangelical Women, Arise!

The motto of Southern Baptists' missionary organization for girls is this passage from the prophet Isaiah:

> Arise, shine, for your light has come,
> and the glory of the LORD shines over you.
> For look, darkness covers the earth,
> and total darkness the peoples;
> but the LORD will shine over you,
> and His glory will appear over you. (Isa. 60:1–2)

Let the genuine evangelical women of the world arise and make themselves known. Theological education, involvement in the hierarchy of the church, endorsement of the Equal Rights Amendment, some career avocation, or membership in the "Evangelical Women's Caucus" is not required. In fact, the latter organization is as far removed from genuine evangelicalism as is possible. Beware of labels and test the spirits!

As one woman, having both master's and doctor's degrees in theological education, I am an "old-fashioned" evangelical in the traditional sense of the term, a woman grateful to God not only for essential equality as His creation but also for the distinctive, God-assigned role that gives me a place in His plan. I gladly accept my primary responsibility as the wife of a preacher-theologian and as the mother of two precious children, who have now taken their places in the next generation—the finest and most challenging opportunity God ever assigned to anyone. No one is any more liberated than a genuine evangelical woman. She is free to know God's Word, and she is committed to do what He requires to the best of her ability. Will the real evangelical women please stand up and be counted?

36

Does a Woman Need Theological Education?

Theology is a compound word simply transliterated from the Greek language with the basic meaning "a word about God." Certainly all God's children ought to study His Word, seeking to know the heavenly Father, to understand His lucid principles of godly living, to discover His solutions to problems and disappointments, and to equip themselves for service in His kingdom. Personally, I do see a need for theological education among women for the following reasons.

To Edify a Woman Spiritually

In Scripture there is an incident recorded that should motivate you to study and master the truths and teachings of the Lord Jesus Christ for personal edification. In Luke 10, Mary of Bethany is contrasted with her sister Martha.

Martha was a good woman, an efficient homemaker, a conscientious hostess; but when she asked the Lord to reprimand her sister Mary for not accepting more responsibility in assisting her in these household matters, Jesus rebuked Martha, reminding her that Mary had "chosen that good part" (v. 42 NKJV) of sitting at His feet and hearing His Word. Even so, through the ages the Lord often has given women the opportunity to study His Word, not while neglecting their household responsibilities, but by avoiding being "distracted" with "her many tasks" (v. 40). In other words, you ought never to neglect spiritual training and preparation—not even for the joy of serving others. Another general admonition to study is found in 2 Timothy 3:14–15:

> But as for you, continue in what you have learned and firmly believed. You know those who taught you, and you know that from childhood you have known the sacred Scriptures, which are able to give you wisdom for salvation through faith in Christ Jesus.

This knowledge of the Word through which you gain understanding concerning salvation is not optional. Psalm 119:11 and 105 demand memorization of the Word because Scripture is the pattern to instruct you in the living of the Christian life.

First Peter 3 is richly relevant for women in every generation, and among the helpful admonitions therein is the reminder of verse 15: "But honor the Messiah as Lord in your hearts. Always be ready to give a defense to anyone who asks you for a reason for the hope that is in you."

To Assist Her Husband

The woman was created for and from the man (1 Cor. 11:8–9) to help, assist, and undergird her own husband in the assignment God has given him. The text reads: "And the LORD God said, *"It is* not good that the man should be alone. I will make him a helper comparable to him" [Hebrew, *'ēzer kenegedo,* literally, "a help like or corresponding to him"] (Gen. 2:18 NKJV). This role is a demanding and rewarding responsibility. God created man with a need for woman. Physically, he craves a lover; mentally, he desires a counterpart; emotionally, he needs a companion; spiritually, he seeks a co-laborer. No man needs a "suitable helper" more than a pastor or any man who seeks to serve the Lord in a ministry position.

The pastor's wife can well be described as a "universal spare part." She must keep her home as a prepared shelter for her family and a ready haven for the needy. She certainly should keep herself attractive in order to draw women to herself through her "living letter" testimony (see 2 Cor. 3:2). She is often called upon for entertainment of "angels unaware," members of her husband's flock, co-laborers in the kingdom's work, church leaders and potential leaders, unsaved men and women from the community. The "First Lady of the parsonage," together with her pastor-husband, also has a unique opportunity to use her potential and creativity, her talents and energies in meaningful ministries.

The most outstanding ministering couple in the New Testament is the team of Aquila and Priscilla, who traveled the apostolic world together, sharing the gospel of Christ and expounding the Word of God more fully (Acts 18:2–3, 18, 26).

Priscilla must have been a diligent and discerning student of the Word of God, or she could never have made an impression on the learned Apollos.

Obviously, Priscilla was encouraged by her husband Aquila to take an active part in ministry. When a godly wife is all she ought to be, she completes, complements, and extends her husband; and their joint ministry reaches beyond what either of them could do alone (Ps. 43:4). Paul commends *both of them* as "my coworkers in Christ Jesus" (Rom. 16:3).

When Paige Patterson invited me to link my life with his in marriage, irrevocably and inseparably, he asked me to join him in study and preparation just as long as God kept that door of opportunity open. I have been grateful for the formal studies of seminary, but how much more does my heart overflow with thanksgiving for the hours my husband and I have spent together, studying the Word in preparation for the resulting multifarious ministry God has given us.

Husbands need to encourage their wives to learn. Note 1 Timothy 2:11: "A woman should learn in silence with full submission." The context of this passage indicates that the divine blueprint calls for the husband's encouragement of his wife's learning and teaching. The word translated "silence" (Greek, *hēsuchia*) is literally an attitude of "quietness, calmness, tranquility," in contrast to the descriptive word used by the apostle Paul in 1 Corinthians 14:34 (Greek, *sigatōsan*, literally "stop talking"). This indicates the responsibility of husbands to encourage their wives in learning and suggests the opportunity of wives to acquire knowledge.

To Rear Children in the Lord

Train up a child in the way he should go,
And when he is old he will not depart from it.
(Prov. 22:6 NKJV)

Throughout history, from the establishment of the home in the garden of Eden until the present, women have uniquely shared in producing successive generations, nurturing and sheltering life in the womb until the child's birth and subsequent training, as well as care through childhood, and then supervising the molding of the youth into adulthood. This task alone is important enough to demand a woman's thorough preparation in biblical and theological studies. What a difference in the coming generation if from childhood they were taught by parents and grandparents the Word of God through family worship and individual instruction as a supplement to the Christian education of the church (Deut. 6:4–12).

Nowhere in God's creation should there be a more precise and vivid theological textbook than the Christian home. Certainly with every passing day the home should offer "a word about God" to those within the family circle and to the world looking in. Grandmother Lois and mother Eunice diligently and zealously taught young Timothy, passing on to him the "sincere faith" (2 Tim. 1:5).

To Teach the Younger Women

In the same way, older [i.e., the spiritually mature] women are to be reverent in behavior, not slanderers, not addicted to much wine. They are to teach what is good, so they may encourage the young women to love their husbands and to love their children, to be self-controlled, pure, homemakers, kind, and submissive to their husbands, so that God's message will not be slandered. (Titus 2:3–5)

The pattern for womanhood, the design for marriage, and the blueprint for the home have been severely distorted through the years. Especially in recent years, women are clamoring for more authority and for pastoral leadership roles in the church. However, in Scripture, the role of the woman in the church is pointedly based upon God's divine order for the home—submission to and honor of the husband by the wife. Whether in teaching biblical truth, extending Christian hospitality, or engaging in individual ministries, a woman must always work within the clear authority of God's Word, neither seeking recognition nor demanding higher office, but making every effort to serve Him who is Lord and trusting the providence of God to open opportunities and give usefulness beyond human limitation and expectations.

Certainly, unless the direction of womanhood is turned back to the divine design, ground will be lost continually in the home. What greater reward could a spiritually mature woman find than passing on to other women lessons in biblical womanhood and lessons in Christlike character? There emphatically is *not* direction or permission given to women to occupy a ruling position in the church (1 Tim. 2:12) or to seek ordination from the church. Those in church leadership are called upon to rule their own houses, which if directed to women, would be in direct opposition to the creation order found in the Old Testament and to the New Testament pattern (1 Tim. 3:1–4).

Criterion for Theological Education

You cannot evaluate theological education without determining the criterion that is to test the foundation for such educational pursuits.

The Authority for the Criterion

Theological education must be based upon and measured against the veracity and accuracy of God's Word. There is no better protection and safeguard for doctrinal solidarity than the unquestioned authority of Scripture. Not only must the Bible be the supreme textbook, but also its doctrines must be presented candidly and completely (see 2 Tim. 3:16; Heb. 4:12) to enable a woman to give sound reasons for holding the evangelical view of Scripture and of the gospel as over against various other views.

The Diversity of Exposure

Biblical studies include many areas—New Testament, Old Testament, theology, ethics, church history, Greek, Hebrew, homiletics, and the like. Thus, theological education should have a broad foundation in exposing the student to a well-rounded program of preparing for life and its challenges (2 Tim. 2:15).

Development of an Area of Specialization

Working from a broad general foundation, you must develop your own unique interest without conforming rigidly to any single pattern that would actually inhibit effective education (see 1 Tim. 4:12–16; Eph. 4:7; Rom. 12:3–8). The assignment of spiritual gifts is made by the Creator Himself to enable all members of the "body" of Christ to work together harmoniously and effectively.

Correlation of Knowledge and Practice

You must correlate the theoretical and the pragmatic aspects of education in order to enable you to emerge with the capacity for accomplishing goals for learning through practical exercise based upon a carefully evaluated philosophical foundation (see James 1:22; Col. 2:8). Learning must go hand in hand with the laboratory of actual experience. Every Christian has the privilege and duty to share in the evangelization of the world and to participate in the work of the kingdom. The accoutrements of pedagogy are to be blended within your sphere of life to enhance the discharge of those duties (see 2 Tim. 2:15).

Faculty/Student Interaction

Education involves the interaction of both professional contingency and classroom peers with the student in the classroom. A woman learns much from a mentor merely by being around her, observing her actions and reactions, noting how she deals with problems (Prov. 1:5; 9:9). There should be time for question/answer interaction and for an opportunity to experiment with your own ideas under the pressure of defending a position with your colleagues.

Sources of Theological Education

1. Personal Bible study with the aid of evangelical books and commentaries.

2. Enrollment in correspondence courses or use of electronic resources by scholarly teachers and pastors.
3. Seminars or conferences held in local churches or retreat centers.
4. Study of articles in current evangelical journals and periodicals as well as books penned by godly women and men.
5. Classroom study available in a nearby seminary or Bible college.

Conclusion

In summary, what could be a better background than a strong biblical foundation for any endeavor a young woman might wish to pursue? In the humble opinion of this writer, husbands (not only pastors but businessmen and educators as well) should be encouraged to make every effort to enable their wives to study the truths of God's Word, if not in the classroom or by correspondence, in whatever setting and with whatever resources are available. Yes, theological education is for women, too!

Daily Bible
Reading Plan

Daily Reading Plan

You can read through the Bible in many different ways:

- Select a book in the Old Testament, followed by one in the New Testament, determining your own order.
- Follow one of many structured plans like the one provided here.
- Include a thread of "comfort," as do I, in the midst of whatever your overall plan may be. I try to read a chapter from the book of Proverbs daily (fits nicely into a monthly plan with its 31 chapters) and through the book of Psalms each month (approximately 5 psalms daily).
- I like to savor the passage and meditate upon the words in my reading, marking important phrases and verses, and making notations in my Bible as I do devotional reading so that my heart rather than the reading plan itself is guiding.
- Scripture memory, and even pulling in great hymns of the faith for inspiration, will also enrich your personal devotional time.

Date	Morning	Evening
	❀ *January* ❀	
1	Genesis 1, 2	Matthew 1
2	Genesis 3, 4, 5	Matthew 2
3	Genesis 6, 7, 8	Matthew 3
4	Genesis 9, 10, 11	Matthew 4
5	Genesis 12, 13, 14	Matthew 5:1–26
6	Genesis 15, 16, 17	Matthew 5:27–45
7	Genesis 18, 19	Matthew 6
8	Genesis 20, 21, 22	Matthew 7
9	Genesis 23, 24	Matthew 8
10	Genesis 25, 26	Matthew 9:1–17
11	Genesis 27, 28	Matthew 9:18–38
12	Genesis 29, 30	Matthew 10:1–23
13	Genesis 31, 32	Matthew 10:24–42
14	Genesis 33, 34, 35	Matthew 11
15	Genesis 36, 37	Matthew 12:1–21
16	Genesis 38, 39, 40	Matthew 12:22–50
17	Genesis 41	Matthew 13:1–32
18	Genesis 42, 43	Matthew 13:33–58
19	Genesis 44, 45	Matthew 14:1–21
20	Genesis 46, 47, 48	Matthew 14:22–36
21	Genesis 49, 50	Matthew 15:1–20
22	Exodus 1, 2, 3	Matthew 15:21–39
23	Exodus 4, 5, 6	Matthew 16
24	Exodus 7, 8	Matthew 17
25	Exodus 9, 10	Matthew 18:1–20
26	Exodus 11, 12	Matthew 18:21–35
27	Exodus 13, 14, 15	Matthew 19:1–15
28	Exodus 16, 17, 18	Matthew 19:16–30
29	Exodus 19, 20, 21	Matthew 20:1–16
30	Exodus 22, 23, 24	Matthew 20:17–34
31	Exodus 25, 26	Matthew 21:1–22

❧ *February* ❧

Date	Morning	Evening
1	Exodus 27, 28	Matthew 21:23–46
2	Exodus 29, 30	Matthew 22:1–22
3	Exodus 31, 32, 33	Matthew 22:23–46
4	Exodus 34, 35, 36	Matthew 23:1–22
5	Exodus 37, 38	Matthew 23:23–39
6	Exodus 39, 40	Matthew 24:1–22
7	Leviticus 1, 2, 3	Matthew 24:23–51
8	Leviticus 4, 5, 6	Matthew 25:1–30
9	Leviticus 7, 8, 9	Matthew 25:31–30
10	Leviticus 10, 11, 12	Matthew 26:1–19
11	Leviticus 13	Matthew 26:20–54
12	Leviticus 14	Matthew 26:55–75
13	Leviticus 15, 16, 17	Matthew 27:1–31
14	Leviticus 18, 19	Matthew 27:32–66
15	Leviticus 20, 21	Matthew 28:1–20
16	Leviticus 22, 23	Mark 1:1–22
17	Leviticus 24, 25	Mark 1:23–45
18	Leviticus 26, 27	Mark 2
19	Numbers 1, 2	Mark 3:1–21
20	Numbers 3, 4	Mark 3:22–35
21	Numbers 5, 6	Mark 4:1–20
22	Numbers 7	Mark 4:21–41
23	Numbers 8, 9, 10	Mark 5:1–20
24	Numbers 11, 12, 13	Mark 5:21–43
25	Numbers 14, 15	Mark 6:1–32
26	Numbers 16, 17	Mark 6:33–56
27	Numbers 18, 19, 20	Mark 7:1–13
28	Numbers 21, 22	Mark 7:14–37
29	Numbers 23, 24, 25	Mark 8:1–21

Divide chapters for February 29 and read them February 28 and March 1 when February has only 28 days.

	🌸 *March* 🌸	
Date	*Morning*	*Evening*
1	Numbers 26, 27	Mark 8:22–38
2	Numbers 28, 29	Mark 9:1–29
3	Numbers 30, 31	Mark 9:30–50
4	Numbers 32, 33	Mark 10:1–31
5	Numbers 34, 35, 36	Mark 10:32–52
6	Deuteronomy 1, 2	Mark 11:1–19
7	Deuteronomy 3, 4	Mark 11:20–33
8	Deuteronomy 5, 6, 7	Mark 12:1–27
9	Deuteronomy 8, 9, 10	Mark 12:28–44
10	Deuteronomy 11, 12, 13	Mark 13:1–13
11	Deuteronomy 14, 15, 16	Mark 13:14–37
12	Deuteronomy 17, 18, 19	Mark 14:1–25
13	Deuteronomy 20, 21, 22	Mark 14:25–50
14	Deuteronomy 23, 24, 25	Mark 14:51–72
15	Deuteronomy 26, 27	Mark 15:1–26
16	Deuteronomy 28	Mark 15:27–47
17	Deuteronomy 29, 30	Mark 16
18	Deuteronomy 31, 32	Luke 1:1–23
19	Deuteronomy 33, 34	Luke 1:24–56
20	Joshua 1, 2, 3	Luke 1:57–80
21	Joshua 4, 5, 6	Luke 2:1–24
22	Joshua 7, 8	Luke 2:25–52
23	Joshua 9, 10	Luke 3
24	Joshua 11, 12, 13	Luke 4:1–32
25	Joshua 14, 15	Luke 4:33–44
26	Joshua 16, 17, 18	Luke 5:1–16
27	Joshua 19, 20	Luke 5:17–39
28	Joshua 21, 22	Luke 6:1–26
29	Joshua 23, 24	Luke 6:27–49
30	Judges 1, 2	Luke 7:1–30
31	Judges 3, 4, 5	Luke 7:31–60

Date	Morning	Evening
	🌸 *April* 🌸	
1	Judges 6, 7	Luke 8:1–21
2	Judges 8, 9	Luke 8:22–56
3	Judges 10, 11	Luke 9:1–36
4	Judges 12, 13, 14	Luke 9:37–62
5	Judges 15, 16, 17	Luke 10:1–24
6	Judges 18, 19	Luke 10:25–42
7	Judges 20, 21	Luke 11:1–28
8	Ruth 1, 2, 3, 4	Luke 11:29–54
9	1 Samuel 1, 2, 3	Luke 12:1–34
10	1 Samuel 4, 5, 6	Luke 12:35–59
11	1 Samuel 7, 8, 9	Luke 13:1–21
12	1 Samuel 10, 11, 12	Luke 13:22–35
13	1 Samuel 13, 14	Luke 14:1–24
14	1 Samuel 15, 16	Luke 14:25–35
15	1 Samuel 17, 18	Luke 15:1–10
16	1 Samuel 19, 20, 21	Luke 15:11–32
17	1 Samuel 22, 23, 24	Luke 16:1–18
18	1 Samuel 25, 26	Luke 16:19–31
19	1 Samuel 27, 28, 29	Luke 17:1–19
20	1 Samuel 30, 31	Luke 17:20–37
21	2 Samuel 1, 2, 3	Luke 18:1–17
22	2 Samuel 4, 5, 6	Luke 18:18–43
23	2 Samuel 7, 8, 9	Luke 19:1–28
24	2 Samuel 10, 11, 12	Luke 19:29–48
25	2 Samuel 13, 14	Luke 20:1–26
26	2 Samuel 15, 16	Luke 20:27–47
27	2 Samuel 17, 18	Luke 21:1–19
28	2 Samuel 19, 20	Luke 21:20–38
29	2 Samuel 21, 22	Luke 22:1–30
30	2 Samuel 23, 24	Luke 22:31–53

Date	Morning	Evening
\&t	*May* \&t	
1	1 Kings 1, 2	Luke 22:54–71
2	1 Kings 3, 4, 5	Luke 23:1–26
3	1 Kings 6, 7	Luke 23:27–38
4	1 Kings 8, 9	Luke 23:39–56
5	1 Kings 10, 11	Luke 24:1–35
6	1 Kings 12, 13	Luke 24:36–53
7	1 Kings 14, 15	John 1:1–28
8	1 Kings 16, 17, 18	John 1:29–51
9	1 Kings 19, 20	John 2
10	1 Kings 21, 22	John 3:1–21
11	2 Kings 1, 2, 3	John 3:22–36
12	2 Kings 4, 5	John 4:1–30
13	2 Kings 6, 7, 8	John 4:31–54
14	2 Kings 9, 10, 11	John 5:1–24
15	2 Kings 12, 13, 14	John 5:25–47
16	2 Kings 15, 16, 17	John 6:1–21
17	2 Kings 18, 19	John 6:22–44
18	2 Kings 20, 21, 22	John 6:45–71
19	2 Kings 23, 24, 25	John 7:1–31
20	1 Chronicles 1, 2	John 7:32–53
21	1 Chronicles 3, 4, 5	John 8:1–20
22	1 Chronicles 6, 7	John 8:21–36
23	1 Chronicles 8, 9, 10	John 8:37–59
24	1 Chronicles 11, 12, 13	John 9:1–23
25	1 Chronicles 14, 15, 16	John 9:24–41
26	1 Chronicles 17, 18, 19	John 10:1–21
27	1 Chronicles 20, 21, 22	John 10:22–42
28	1 Chronicles 23, 24, 25	John 11:1–17
29	1 Chronicles 26, 27	John 11:18–46
30	1 Chronicles 28, 29	John 11:47–57
31	2 Chronicles 1, 2, 3	John 12:1–19

	🐦 *June* 🐦	
Date	**Morning**	**Evening**
1	2 Chronicles 4, 5, 6	John 12:20–50
2	2 Chronicles 7, 8, 9	John 13:1–17
3	2 Chronicles 10, 11, 12	John 13:18–38
4	2 Chronicles 13–16	John 14
5	2 Chronicles 17, 18, 19	John 15
6	2 Chronicles 20, 21, 22	John 16:1–15
7	2 Chronicles 23, 24, 25	John 16:16–33
8	2 Chronicles 26, 27, 28	John 17
9	2 Chronicles 29, 30, 31	John 18:1–23
10	2 Chronicles 32, 33	John 18:24–40
11	2 Chronicles 34, 35, 36	John 19:1–22
12	Ezra 1, 2	John 19:23–42
13	Ezra 3, 4, 5	John 20
14	Ezra 6, 7, 8	John 21
15	Ezra 9, 10	Acts 1
16	Nehemiah 1, 2, 3	Acts 2:1–13
17	Nehemiah 4, 5, 6	Acts 2:14–47
18	Nehemiah 7, 8	Acts 3
19	Nehemiah 9, 10, 11	Acts 4:1–22
20	Nehemiah 12, 13	Acts 4:23–37
21	Esther 1, 2, 3	Acts 5:1–16
22	Esther 4, 5, 6	Acts 5:17–42
23	Esther 7–10	Acts 6
24	Job 1, 2, 3	Acts 7:1–19
25	Job 4, 5, 6	Acts 7:20–43
26	Job 7, 8, 9	Acts 7:44–60
27	Job 10, 11, 12	Acts 8:1–25
28	Job 13, 14, 15	Acts 8:26–40
29	Job 16, 17, 18	Acts 9:1–22
30	Job 19, 20	Acts 9:23–43

❦ July ❦

Date	Morning	Evening
1	Job 21, 22	Acts 10:1–23
2	Job 23, 24, 25	Acts 10:24–48
3	Job 26, 27, 28	Acts 11
4	Job 29, 30	Acts 12
5	Job 31, 32	Acts 13:1–23
6	Job 33, 34	Acts 13:24–52
7	Job 35, 36, 37	Acts 14
8	Job 38, 39	Acts 15:1–21
9	Job 40, 41, 42	Acts 15:22–41
10	Psalms 1, 2, 3	Acts 16:1–15
11	Psalms 4, 5, 6	Acts 16:16–40
12	Psalms 7, 8, 9	Acts 17:1–15
13	Psalms 10, 11, 12	Acts 17:16–34
14	Psalms 13–16	Acts 18
15	Psalms 17, 18	Acts 19:1–20
16	Psalms 19, 20, 21	Acts 19:21–41
17	Psalms 22, 23, 24	Acts 20:1–16
18	Psalms 25, 26, 27	Acts 20:17–38
19	Psalms 28, 29, 30	Acts 21:1–14
20	Psalms 31, 32, 33	Acts 21:15–40
21	Psalms 34, 35	Acts 22
22	Psalms 36, 37	Acts 23:1–11
23	Psalms 38, 39, 40	Acts 23:12–35
24	Psalms 41, 42, 43	Acts 24
25	Psalms 44, 45, 46	Acts 25
26	Psalms 47, 48, 49	Acts 26
27	Psalms 50, 51, 52	Acts 27:1–25
28	Psalms 53, 54, 55	Acts 27:26–44
29	Psalms 56, 57, 58	Acts 28:1–15
30	Psalms 59, 60, 61	Acts 28:16–31
31	Psalms 62, 63, 64	Romans 1

✤ *August* ✤

Date	Morning	Evening
1	Psalms 65, 66, 67	Romans 2
2	Psalms 68, 69	Romans 3
3	Psalms 70, 71, 72	Romans 4
4	Psalms 73, 74	Romans 5
5	Psalms 75, 76, 77	Romans 6
6	Psalm 78	Romans 7
7	Psalms 79, 80, 81	Romans 8:1–18
8	Psalms 82, 83, 84	Romans 8:19–39
9	Psalms 85, 86, 87	Romans 9
10	Psalms 88, 89	Romans 10
11	Psalms 90, 91, 92	Romans 11:1–21
12	Psalms 93, 94, 95	Romans 11:22–36
13	Psalms 96, 97, 98	Romans 12
14	Psalms 99–102	Romans 13
15	Psalms 103, 104	Romans 14
16	Psalms 105, 106	Romans 15:1–20
17	Psalms 107, 108	Romans 15:21–33
18	Psalms 109, 110, 111	Romans 16
19	Psalms 112–115	1 Corinthians 1
20	Psalms 116–118	1 Corinthians 2
21	Psalms 119:1–48	1 Corinthians 3
22	Psalms 119:49–104	1 Corinthians 4
23	Psalms 119:105–175	1 Corinthians 5
24	Psalms 120–123	1 Corinthians 6
25	Psalms 124–127	1 Corinthians 7:1–24
26	Psalms 125–131	1 Corinthians 7:25–40
27	Psalms 132–135	1 Corinthians 8
28	Psalms 136–138	1 Corinthians 9
29	Psalms 139–141	1 Corinthians 10:1–13
30	Psalms 142–144	1 Corinthians 10:14–33
31	Psalms 145–147	1 Corinthians 11:1–15

Date	Morning	Evening
❧ September ❧		
1	Psalms 148–150	1 Corinthians 11:16–34
2	Proverbs 1, 2	1 Corinthians 12
3	Proverbs 3, 4	1 Corinthians 13
4	Proverbs 5, 6	1 Corinthians 14:1–20
5	Proverbs 7, 8	1 Corinthians 14:21–40
6	Proverbs 9, 10	1 Corinthians 15:1–32
7	Proverbs 11, 12	1 Corinthians 15:33–58
8	Proverbs 13, 14	1 Corinthians 16
9	Proverbs 15, 16	2 Corinthians 1
10	Proverbs 17, 18	2 Corinthians 2
11	Proverbs 19, 20	2 Corinthians 3
12	Proverbs 21, 22	2 Corinthians 4
13	Proverbs 23, 24	2 Corinthians 5
14	Proverbs 25, 26, 27	2 Corinthians 6
15	Proverbs 28, 29	2 Corinthians 7
16	Proverbs 30, 31	2 Corinthians 8
17	Ecclesiastes 1, 2, 3	2 Corinthians 9
18	Ecclesiastes 4, 5, 6	2 Corinthians 10
19	Ecclesiastes 7, 8, 9	2 Corinthians 11:1–15
20	Ecclesiastes 10, 11, 12	2 Corinthians 11:16–33
21	Song of Solomon 1, 2, 3	2 Corinthians 12
22	Song of Solomon 4, 5	2 Corinthians 13
23	Song of Solomon 6, 7, 8	Galatians 1
24	Isaiah 1, 2, 3	Galatians 2
25	Isaiah 4, 5, 6	Galatians 3
26	Isaiah 7, 8, 9	Galatians 4
27	Isaiah 10, 11, 12	Galatians 5
28	Isaiah 13, 14, 15	Galatians 6
29	Isaiah 16, 17, 18	Ephesians 1
30	Isaiah 19, 20, 21	Ephesians 2

❦ *October* ❦

Date	Morning	Evening
1	Isaiah 22, 23	Ephesians 3
2	Isaiah 24, 25, 26	Ephesians 4
3	Isaiah 27, 28	Ephesians 5
4	Isaiah 29, 30	Ephesians 6
5	Isaiah 31, 32, 33	Philippians 1
6	Isaiah 34, 35, 36	Philippians 2
7	Isaiah 37, 38	Philippians 3
8	Isaiah 39, 40	Philippians 4
9	Isaiah 41, 42	Colossians 1
10	Isaiah 43, 44	Colossians 2
11	Isaiah 45, 46, 47	Colossians 3
12	Isaiah 48, 49	Colossians 4
13	Isaiah 50, 51, 52	1 Thessalonians 1
14	Isaiah 53, 54, 55	1 Thessalonians 2
15	Isaiah 56, 57, 58	1 Thessalonians 3
16	Isaiah 59, 60, 61	1 Thessalonians 4
17	Isaiah 61, 63, 64	1 Thessalonians 5
18	Isaiah 65, 66	2 Thessalonians 1
19	Jeremiah 1, 2	2 Thessalonians 2
20	Jeremiah 3, 4	2 Thessalonians 3
21	Jeremiah 5, 6	1 Timothy 1
22	Jeremiah 7, 8	1 Timothy 2
23	Jeremiah 9, 10	1 Timothy 3
24	Jeremiah 11, 12, 13	1 Timothy 4
25	Jeremiah 14, 15, 16	1 Timothy 5
26	Jeremiah 17, 18, 19	1 Timothy 6
27	Jeremiah 20, 21, 22	2 Timothy 1
28	Jeremiah 23, 24	2 Timothy 2
29	Jeremiah 25, 26	2 Timothy 3
30	Jeremiah 27, 28	2 Timothy 4
31	Jeremiah 29, 30	Titus 1

🌸 *November* 🌸		
Date	**Morning**	**Evening**
1	Jeremiah 31, 32	Titus 2
2	Jeremiah 33, 34, 35	Titus 3
3	Jeremiah 36, 37	Philemon
4	Jeremiah 38, 39	Hebrews 1
5	Jeremiah 40, 41, 42	Hebrews 2
6	Jeremiah 43, 44, 45	Hebrews 3
7	Jeremiah 46, 47, 48	Hebrews 4
8	Jeremiah 49, 50	Hebrews 5
9	Jeremiah 51, 52	Hebrews 6
10	Lamentations 1, 2	Hebrews 7
11	Lamentations 3, 4, 5	Hebrews 8
12	Ezekiel 1, 2, 3	Hebrews 9
13	Ezekiel 4, 5, 6	Hebrews 10:1–23
14	Ezekiel 7, 8, 9	Hebrews 10:24–39
15	Ezekiel 10, 11, 12	Hebrews 11:1–19
16	Ezekiel 13, 14, 15	Hebrews 11:20–40
17	Ezekiel 16	Hebrews 12
18	Ezekiel 17, 18, 19	Hebrews 13
19	Ezekiel 20, 21	James 1
20	Ezekiel 22, 23	James 2
21	Ezekiel 24, 25, 26	James 3
22	Ezekiel 27, 28	James 4
23	Ezekiel 29, 30, 31	James 5
24	Ezekiel 32, 33	1 Peter 1
25	Ezekiel 34, 35	1 Peter 2
26	Ezekiel 36, 37	1 Peter 3
27	Ezekiel 38, 39	1 Peter 4
28	Ezekiel 40	1 Peter 5
29	Ezekiel 41, 42	2 Peter 1
30	Ezekiel 43, 44	2 Peter 2

Date	Morning	Evening
	🐚 *December* 🐚	
1	Ezekiel 45, 46	2 Peter 3
2	Ezekiel 47, 48	1 John 1
3	Daniel 1, 2	1 John 2
4	Daniel 3, 4	1 John 3
5	Daniel 5, 6	1 John 4
6	Daniel 7, 8	1 John 5
7	Daniel 9, 10	2 John
8	Daniel 11, 12	3 John
9	Hosea 1–4	Jude
10	Hosea 5–8	Revelation 1
11	Hosea 9, 10, 11	Revelation 2
12	Hosea 12, 13, 14	Revelation 3
13	Joel	Revelation 4
14	Amos 1, 2, 3	Revelation 5
15	Amos 4, 5, 6	Revelation 6
16	Amos 7, 8, 9	Revelation 7
17	Obadiah	Revelation 8
18	Jonah	Revelation 9
19	Micah 1, 2, 3	Revelation 10
20	Micah 4, 5	Revelation 11
21	Micah 6, 7	Revelation 12
22	Nahum	Revelation 13
23	Habakkuk	Revelation 14
24	Zephaniah	Revelation 15
25	Haggai	Revelation 16
26	Zechariah 1–3	Revelation 17
27	Zechariah 4, 5, 6	Revelation 18
28	Zechariah 7, 8, 9	Revelation 19
29	Zechariah 10, 11, 12	Revelation 20
30	Zechariah 13, 14	Revelation 21
31	Malachi	Revelation 22